M.I.A.
ACCOUNTING FOR
THE MISSING
IN SOUTHEAST ASIA

M.I.A.

ACCOUNTING FOR THE MISSING IN SOUTHEAST ASIA

PAUL D. MATHER

1994
National Defense University Press
Washington, DC

National Defense University Press

To increase general knowledge and inform discussion, the Institute for National Strategic Studies, through its publication arm the NDU Press, publishes McNair Papers; proceedings of University- and Institute-sponsored symposia; books relating to U.S. national security, especially to issues of joint, combined, or coalition warfare, peacekeeping operations, and national strategy; and a variety of briefer works designed to circulate contemporary comment and offer alternatives to current policy. The Press occasionally publishes out-of-print defense classics, historical works and other especially timely or distinguished writing on national security.

Opinions, conclusions, and recommendations expressed or implied in this volume are solely those of the author and do not necessarily represent the views of the National Defense University, the Department of Defense, or any other government agency. Cleared for public release, distribution unlimited.

Photographs are by the author, except for the Associated Press photograph on p. 119.

NDU Press publications are sold by the U.S. Government Printing Office. For ordering information, call(202) 783-3238, or write to: Superintendent of Documents, U.S. Government Printing Office

Library of Congress, Cataloging-in-Publication Data
Mather, Paul D., 1938-
    M.I.A. : accounting in Southeast Asia / Paul D. Mather.
     p.   cm.
    Includes index.
    1. Vietnamese Conflicts, 1961-1975—Missing in action—United States. 2. Vietnamese Conflict, 1961-1975—Prisoners and prisons. 3. Prisoners of war—United States. 4. United States—Foreign relations—Indochina. 5. Indochina—Foreign relations—United States. I. Title. II. Title: MIA.
—DS559.8.M5M37   1994
—959.704'31—dc20   94-28928
                                           CIP

First printing, December 1994

For sale by the U.S. Government Printing Office
Superintendent of Documents, Mail Stop:SSOP, Washington, DC 20402-9328
ISBN 0-16-036391-8

CONTENTS

FOREWORD   xi

PREFACE   xiii

THE UNACCOUNTED FOR   xix

CHAPTER 1: THE PARIS PEACE ACCORDS   1
  MIAs and Ending the Conflict   1
  An Uneasy Cease-fire   4
  The Four-Party Joint Military Team   6
  Joint Casualty Resolution Center   10
  JCRC Operations Begin   13
  Sea Salvage Operations   15
  "Public Communications" and the Rewards
    Program   16
  More Casualties and a Changed Concept   20
  A Reduced JCRC   26

CHAPTER 2: A WINDING DOWN   35
  A Period of Malaise   35
  The Role of Congress   40
  The Woodcock Commission   51
  The Move Toward US-Vietnam Normalization   61

CHAPTER 3: HEIGHTENED ACTIVITY   69
  Refugees Stream From Indochina   69
  MIA Reports Flow In   74

The Information Proves Useful   79
Progress Slows   84
The Reagan Inheritance   87
Reorganizing for More Effective Action   89

CHAPTER 4: PRIVATE INVOLVEMENT   95
The National League of Families   95
Other MIA Interest Groups   100
Rise of the "Rambos"   103
Efforts of Untrained Amateurs   109
Attempts by the "Con Artists"   112

CHAPTER 5: RENEWED EFFORTS   123
Establishing and Maintaining Contact   123
Technical Meetings   130
Field Work   133
Uneven Progress   142

CHAPTER 6: TOWARD CASUALTY
RESOLUTION   151
"Creating a Favorable Atmosphere"   151
Special Presidential Emissary   155
The Vessey-Thach Agreements   158
Parallel Progress in Laos   166
1988, Turning the Corner   168
More Recent Progress in Vietnam   170
Movement in Laos and Cambodia   175
Looking Back   177

EPILOGUE   183

GLOSSARY   189

INDEX   193

THE AUTHOR   207

PHOTOGRAPHS

A poster on a tree in Con Tho City solicits
casualty information 19

JCRC members load the flag-covered body of
Captain Richard Rees onto an aircraft in Saigon 24

Members of the House Select Committee on
Missing Persons met with Vietnamese officials in
Hanoi in late 1975 41

This bas-relief on a factory wall in Hanoi reports
the shootdown of an American aircraft 77

Vietnamese citizen Tran Huu Hai (also known as
"Tony" Hai) 105

Peace Corps worker Greg Kamm, who was
misrepresented as an American POW by
unscrupulous individuals in Thailand 113

Mr. Charles Strait, who posed as an American
POW 116

A display of one million dollars in cash,
representing a reward offered for the safe return
of an American POW from Southeast Asia 119

American and Vietnamese workers excavate the
site of a 1972 bomber crash near Hanoi 139

A joint American-Vietnamese team is poled
across a reservoir near Thanh Hoa 144

The SRV repatriated a number of American
remains to US custody at Hanoi's Noi Bai
Airport in April 1986 154

MAP

Mainland Southeast Asia xviii

FOREWORD

Among the numerous analyses of those missing in action in Southeast Asia, this study is the first to concentrate on the *process* whereby the US military tried to resolve each case. Much of the continuing controversy ignores or refuses to accept the fact that the US Government, through the Joint Casualty Resolution Center and other mechanisms, has made a thorough, sustained, good faith effort to determine the fate of every serviceman declared missing in action in that conflict. The author, who spent more than 15 years in Southeast Asia taking part in those endeavors, tells the story of this unique effort from the point of view of an informed insider.

A member of the MIA search team from the early 1970s through the late 1980s, Paul Mather is well qualified to relate the history of this effort. He covers a wide range of topics, from field work at crash sites and personal interchanges with Vietnamese, Cambodian, Lao, and Thai officials, through the various international accords that governed the activities of the US investigatory teams. Although political changes in the United States alternately facilitated or hampered search efforts, the attempt to resolve every case never ceased. Colonel Mather faithfully records the efforts of individuals and organizations that played major roles in this drama: congressional committees; the National League of Families; private citizens who made sincere efforts to help; senior government officials like General John Vessey, who headed a special full-accounting commission; military agencies such as the Joint Casualty Resolution Center and the Army's Central Identification Laboratory; scoundrels and swindlers who exploited the tragedy for personal gain; and self-styled Rambos who acted on their own.

This account should help to wrap up an especially emotional chapter of the Vietnam war. By telling *how* the process worked for almost two decades, it contributes to the full accounting desired by all.

PAUL G. CERJAN
Lieutenant General, US Army
President, National Defense University

PREFACE

As a member of the Joint Casualty Resolution Center (JCRC) from its formation in Saigon in early 1973 until my reassignment back to the continental United States from Bangkok in the fall of 1988, I have had the unique opportunity to occupy a front row seat to events in Southeast Asia. More importantly, I have had the extreme good fortune to have spent over fifteen years as either a participant or a close observer of the US government's efforts to resolve the issue of American servicemen still unaccounted for in Southeast Asia as a consequence of the Vietnam war. For those most directly involved, these efforts always carried with them a sense of urgency, and we were surrounded by co-workers who shared in the dedication and enthuiasm for the task. It was a period of extreme frustration and constant challenge, of numerous disappointments, and only a small measure of progress and success. But by far the most satisfying feature was the knowledge that ours was simply a mission of great humanitarian importance, that of helping determine the fate of our comrades-in-arms. No one who has served in the military could possibly wish for a more fulfilling assignment.

Though since 1975 the United States has had comparatively narrow dealings with the former Indochinese states of Vietnam, Laos, and Cambodia, the issue of the missing in action (MIAs) and the prisoners of war (POWs) has loomed large in our limited intercourse. From the US point of view, this was the main issue left unresolved when direct United States involvement in the Vietnam conflict ended.

Having devoted such a large percentage of my military career to this issue, I find it disturbing to hear the occasional allegations that nothing has been done by the United States to resolve the POW/MIA problem, or that our government has approached this problem with ill intent. Milder criticism, perhaps correct, has implied that there have been periods when opportunities were missed, or when we might have done better, or when we could have gone faster. More severe criticism has alleged that our government was guilty of cover-up and duplicity. But, behind what at times may have seemed to be an unfeeling bureaucracy, in fact there have been very many highly skilled military and civilian officials who have pursued this difficult mission with great dedication, sincerely hoping for ultimate success. My hope is that this simple monograph will shed some light on these efforts, both successful and unsuccessful.

I make no claim that this is an unbiased account. Nor is it, by any stretch of the imagination, in any way a complete account; the US government's POW/MIA activity is much too broad to cover in detail within the scope of this limited study. In addition, my view was limited to that of a member of the JCRC, stationed first in Saigon and later in Bangkok half a world away from the flagpole in Washington DC where many of the decisions were made. There is no doubt that someone working this issue from the Washington DC end would see things differently.

Though the reader may detect a bias toward the role of the JCRC, there is no intent to downplay the role of others. The many elements of the Departments of Defense and State, the Army's Central Identification Laboratory, the Defense Intelligence Agency, the National Security Council, the CIA, the National Security Agency, and even less directly related organizations such as the Drug Enforcement Agency and the FBI, among many others, have contributed in their own way to this task. It is a tribute to our form of government that "the bureaucracy" can unite and generate such a concerted effort to determine the fate of those warriors who did not return to their families following a conflict. The citizenry of most other countries on this planet are not as fortunate.

Readers may also detect greater emphasis on discussion of our interactions with Vietnam, and might question the author's lesser emphasis on Laos and Cambodia. There are several reasons for this. An argument can be made that Vietnam is the "first among equals" of the former Indochinese states, and that any activity on the POW/MIA issue with Vietnam will have a corresponding effect on activity in the other two countries. I happen to subscribe to this argument, and fully expect that as cooperation on this issue improves between the United States and Vietnam, we will see a corresponding increase in cooperation with both Laos and Cambodia. More importantly, however, since the United States had no diplomatic relations with Vietnam—and therefore no embassy or ambassador in Hanoi—those of us in the JCRC often found ourselves acting as intermediaries between our two countries, dealing directly with Vietnamese officials. Thus we had more firsthand and direct knowledge of events relating to the issue. This situation is contrasted with that in Laos where the United States did not break diplomatic relations and has maintained an embassy in Vientiane over the intervening years since the communist takeover of the Lao government. There, the JCRC has played a supporting role, always subordinate to the United States embassy.

In the case of Cambodia, the tragic events there precluded all but the most minimal contact—by any element of the United States government—during the years following the 1975 communist takeover. These factors notwithstanding, the reader should not interpret the author's emphasis on Vietnam as indicative of a lack of governmental concern for those hundreds of servicemen yet unaccounted for in Laos and Cambodia; certainly no slight is intended.

I would like to express my appreciation to the staff of the National Defense University for affording me the opportunity and the environment in which to reflect and write. Particular thanks go to Dr. John Endicott, Dr. Fred Kiley, Dr. Joe Goldberg, and Dr. Dora Alves for their encouragement and assistance. The unsung staff of the NDU Library also deserve my praise for the research assistance so necessary for filling in the many voids in my fading memory. Invaluable assistance was also provided by the staff of the Defense Intelligence Agency (DIA), and the Joint Casualty Resolution Center (JCRC). Both gave me unrestricted access to their files. A special thanks must also go to one who shares my interest in Southeast Asia and who played a special role in advocating this project, Dr. Lewis Stern from the Office of the Assistant Secretary of Defense for International Security Affairs.

Though I have received encouragement and assistance from many friends, the responsibility for all errors, faults, misinterpretations, or shortcomings in this manuscript, is entirely mine.

Finally, I would like to dedicate this book to a group of special people who still suffer, mostly in silence, from the lingering effects of the Vietnam conflict: the families of those still unaccounted for. May their burden be eased someday soon.

PAUL D. MATHER
Washington, DC

M.I.A.
ACCOUNTING FOR
THE MISSING
IN SOUTHEAST ASIA

Mainland Southeast Asia

THE UNACCOUNTED FOR

It is early morning in South Vietnam, Tuesday, the 17th of June, 1969. As the rising sun burns off the haze and chases away the dew and dampness, Private First Class Donald Lee Sparks and the others in his platoon proceed cautiously through the abandoned rice field to the west of Tam Ky. Private Sparks reflects briefly on the contrast between this war-torn and hostile countryside and the peaceful fields of Iowa where he grew up.

Sparks' attention is suddenly attracted to movements off to his right. A Vietnamese man, apparently a woodcutter, briefly appears at the edge of the clearing, then quickly darts away through the underbrush and up toward the top of a nearby rise. Sensing the unusual nature of this behavior, Sparks' platoon warily pursues, and soon comes upon a small thatched hut about halfway up the rise. As PFC Sparks and his teammates reconnoiter the hut, the morning quiet is terrifyingly shattered bythe sudden crack of automatic arms fire from a nearby concealed bunker. Sparks and another man are cut down immediately, both seemingly critically wounded. Under the pressure of intense enemy fire, Sparks' unit is forced to withdraw, unable to either help or retrieve the two wounded men. Sparks is last glimpsed by his retreating teammates as enemy soldiers move into the area and strip his wounded body of his clothing and weapon.

The follwing day, another United States patrol is dispatched to the area to search for the two wounded men left behind. The body of one man is recovered, but there remains absolutely no trace of Private First Class Donald Lee Sparks.[1]

And thus begins another human tragedy. Another American soldier is unaccounted for, a casualty whose fate is uncertain, his exact whereabouts unknown. His loved ones at home will be shocked by that ominous visit to their door by a chaplain and a casualty representative whose unhappy duty it is to provide notification, and the familys' terrible agony will begin. They suffer and grieve, and their hopes may be buoyed—or dashed—as additional information is learned.

Time passes . . . weeks, months, and years . . . and additional information may *not* be forthcoming. For some families there may eventually come a realization that the loss in permanent, that the soldier will not return, that in time of war these terrible things happen. For other families there can be no time of acceptance. The thought of loss is too great, and the hope remains that somehow, someday, they will know, and the uncertainty of it all will finally come to an end.

During the roughly one decade of direct United States military involvement in the conflict in Southeast Asia, nearly 3 million US servicemen served in our armed forces in that theater. The war took a toll of over 58 thousand killed, and 300 thousand wounded.[2] A small number of prisoners were released while the hostilities were still going on, and 591 US prisoners were eventually released and repatriated back to United States control during the emotional Operation Homecoming in early 1973. But there remained over 2,500 servicemen whose fate was yet to be determined: those believed to have been captured but who were not returned with the other prisoners, those known to have been killed but whose remains had not yet been recovered, and those who were missing, with little known about the circumstances. The resolution of these cases, the unaccounted for, was to become—and still remains—the subject of great US concern and continuing intensive governmental effort.

Like the Vietnam war itself, the issue of the missing-in-action is fraught with emotion.[3] It is an issue which has the attention of not only the Executive branch of our government and the families directly concerned, but also of the general public, the media, the congress, and certainly the ultimately victorious communist governments of Indochina. Perhaps at no time in the history of American wars has such an organized effort been mounted to resolve the fate of US servicemen as has occurred in the case of the Vietnam War.[4] The effort has drawn praise and even admiration from some quarters, while at the same time prompting accusations of cover-up, duplicity, and inaction on the part of the US government. Much has been written and much has been said about the MIAs, but there still exists considerable misinformation and no small amount of disinformation. The issue of American servicemen still unaccounted for as a result of our longest war has brought out the emotional best in many Americans and—unfortunately—the worst ina few. The emotionalism of the issue is exemplified by such charged headlines as "EX-CONGRESSMAN LEBOU-TILLIER CALLS U.S. EFFORTS ON MIAS 'PA-THETIC' "[5] or "MIA ISSUE: PEROT BLAMES GOV'T FOR SLOW PROGRESS,[6] or such catchy quotes as the following, attributed to would-be POW rescuer and former Green Beret officer James "Bo" Gritz: " . . . But I'm afraid that only God, the mothers, the wives who remained true, and the Special Forces want the prisoners back."[7]

Despite the controversy implied by such headlines, agreement is unanimous that the effort to resolve the fate of our missing is unquestionably a proper obligation of the US government. This is so, not only for very pragmatic military reasons, but also because it accords with the American values and traditions for which these servicemen fought and sacrificed. In recent years efforts to resolve the MIA issue have enjoyed consistent bipartisan support in Congress, and have become a matter of high national priority within the Executive branch and its associated agencies and departments. On innumerable occasions the President and other government officials have reaffirmed to the American public and, more importantly, to the families themselves, a continuing commitment to achieve the fullest possible accounting for those still unaccounted for as a result of the hostilities in Indochina.

NOTES

1. The details of the incident involving PFC Sparks were extracted from unclassified DIA and JCRC summary files.

2. These casualty figures, obtained from Department of Defense documents, like many of the statistics associated with the Vietnam conflict, lack precision and are therefore subject to further refinement or qualification.

3. Strictly speaking, the term "missing-in-action" or "MIA" carries a legal connotation implying that the service member still lives. As used herein, the author accepts the more common use of the term which implies that the member is still unaccounted for.

4. Indeed, there is still an on-going government effort to resolve the fate of casualties from previous wars, particularly those from World War II and the Korean War. The mechanism for this effort, however, is by comparison very straightforward and routine. This effort does not involve such a complexity of organizations, and does not bear the weight of emotion as US effort to resolve Vietnam War casualties.

5. Headline for an article which appeared in the *New York City Tribune*, 3 April 1986, written by staff members Evans Johnson and Patrick J. Martin. The article describes criticism leveled against United States POW/MIA resolution efforts by John Leboutillier, former Republican Congressman from New York.

6. Headline of a UPI article which appeared in the English-language Bangkok newspaper, *The Nation Review*, dated 26 April 1987. The article reports comments made by Texas billionaire businessman H. Ross Perot who has maintained a continuing interest in the POW/MIA issue.

7. Quoted from an interview of James Gritz (LTC, Ret), which was published in the March 1982 issue of *Penthouse*. Gritz, a former Special Forces officer, has gained a great deal of notoriety because of his claimed knowledge of American captives held in Indochina, and because of his alleged forays into Laos to rescue these Americans.

1

THE PARIS PEACE ACCORDS

MIAs AND ENDING THE CONFLICT

President Nixon began his first term of office with
a clear mandate to disengage from the Vietnam conflict.
US efforts in this regard proved to be extremely slow
and agonizing. At the time of the transition between the
Johnson and Nixon administrations in January 1969, the
so-called plenary peace talks which had recently convened
in Paris between the parties to the conflict had achieved
little except an agreement on the shape of the negotiating
table. Nevertheless, these talks proceeded, generally with
precious few tangible results except to provide the North
Vietnamese delegates with a forum in which to tutor the
US negotiators in the nuances of Vietnamese communist
negotiation "logic."[1] Such logic included stalling tactics,
disagreements about agenda, portraying a position of
flexibility to visitors and the media while maintaining a
rigid stance against the United States negotiators, and
other "psychological" ploys.

As with any negotiation effort, each of the parties
brought to Paris their own ideas of what was to be
achieved. The American side was seeking, among other

things, a cessation of the hostilities in Vietnam, guarantees of peaceful reconciliation, withdrawal of US combat forces from the conflict, and the return of American prisoners of war. Some of these items would be opposed by the Viet Cong and North Vietnamese participants; others would be welcomed. A key element of the US negotiation strategy was to maintain the legitimacy of the non-communist government of South Vietnam, our ally. It was judged that to seek anything less would be to jeopardize US honor and prestige and, ultimately, US credibility as a reliable ally and effective leader in the free world. This issue became the big sticking point of the negotiations that delayed agreement on ending the war.

The plenary talks in Paris plodded onward ineffectually at a glacial pace. Meanwhile, behind these overt sessions a series of secret meetings beginning in August 1969 between North Vietnamese officials and then National Security Adviser Henry Kissinger took place.[2] These secret negotiations, finally made public by Nixon in January 1972 in an attempt to quell the outcries of anti-war activists, eventually became the vehicle by which the final terms of agreement on settling the conflict were hammered out between the United States and the Democratic Republic of Vietnam (North Vietnam).

The issue of missing American servicemen figured prominently (usually as it applied to the prisoners of war) in the conduct of these laborious negotiations. North Vietnamese officials had taken an extremely tough negotiating stance on this particular matter, knowing full well the emotionalism of the issue. Initially, they had called for complete withdrawal of US troops from Vietnam as a precondition for the release of the prisoners. Meanwhile, the negotiators in Paris, both American and North Vietnamese, were besieged by groups of visiting family members of servicemen held prisoner or listed as missing. The activities of these groups served to remind the US negotiators of the families' expectation that this issue would be an integral part of the peace settlement. Unfortunately, these activities also reinforced the North Vietnamese perception that the issue of missing Americans was a bargaining chip that could extract further concessions from the US side.

Not until after their 1972 Easter offensive ground to a halt did the North Vietnamese show indications of a willingness to seriously negotiate an end to the conflict. Discussions began again in July 1972 in Paris between Dr. Kissinger and North Vietnamese negotiator Le Duc Tho, and thereafter proceeded haltingly toward a final conclusion and written agreement in January 1973. Only during this final fitful thrust toward a negotiated end to the conflict did the North Vietnamese back away from their earlier precondition and agree that the release of American prisoners would take place simultaneously with the United States troop withdrawal.

Ultimately, the agreements called for, among other things, the cessation of hostilities, the withdrawal of US troops, the dismantling of bases and the clearing of mines, the return of captured and detained military and civilian personnel, a reconciliation among the Vietnamese parties, and the establishment of a mechanism of commissions and teams to carry out, control, and supervise the implementation of the accords and their various protocols.

In addition to the question of prisoners of war, the final negotiations also addressed the issue of Americans still missing and unaccounted for. The negotiators on both sides were aware that the return of those servicemen held prisoner would not clear up the issue of missing service members. Our knowledge of exactly what had happened to each missing individual varied over the entire spectrum, from precise knowledge at one extreme to absolutely no knowledge at the other. At the same time, there was abundant proof that the communist side had to know, at some level within their government, the fate of many of these missing individuals. During the course of the conflict, the DRV had published, on a number of occasions, photos of identifiable personal effects of Americans—ID cards, Geneva Convention cards, and so on— as well as other equally convincing indications that they had knowledge of missing Americans. Therefore, some provision needed to be made for resolution of these unanswered questions upon cessation of the hostilities. The visits of family members to Paris during the negotiations, as noted earlier, served to keep the pressure on the authors of the final accords and to ensure that these interests were considered and dealt with.

In Paris on 27 January 1973, representatives of the Democratic Republic of Vietnam (DRV, the North Vietnamese government), the Provisional Revolutionary Government of the Republic of South Vietnam (PRG, the "Viet Cong" shadow government in South Vietnam), the government of the Republic of Vietnam (RVN, the government of our ally in South Vietnam), and the United States of America signed a document officially titled "The Agreement on Ending the War and Restoring Peace in Vietnam." This document, more commonly referred to as the Paris Accords, included as a specific provision an article dealing with the resolution of the fate of those Americans (and others) still unaccounted for at the conclusion of the hostilities. Article 8(b), states:

> The parties shall help each other to get information about those military personnel and foreign civilians of the parties missing in action, to determine the location and take care of the graves of the dead so as to facilitate the exhumation and repatriation of the remains, and to take any such other measures as may be required to get information about those still considered missing in action.

Thus, at 2400 hours GMT on 27 January 1973 the stage was unknowingly set for what was to become a most difficult, frustrating, trying, and exceedingly lengthy effort to carry out the provisions of Article 8(b) of the Paris Accords and to determine the fate of our missing men.

AN UNEASY CEASE-FIRE

The morning of 28 January 1973 in Saigon was warm and sunny, and in the streets was the usual Sunday bustle of traffic. There appeared to be little outward indication, however, that this was an auspicious day—the beginning of an official cease-fire after so many long years of war. Strangely, the populace seemed to take little note, and there was no particular air of euphoria or celebration. A Vietnamese Air Force C–47 droned in slow circles overhead, spewing leaflets which fluttered slowly down to the city's inhabitants. These leaflets announced the cease-fire but, prophetically, also exhorted the citizenry to maintain their vigilance against expected deceptions by a devious enemy. Quite obviously the government of Vietnam, our ally, had no illusions about the character of the two communist signatories, the DRV and the PRG, nor did they put much stock in the assurances written into the Paris Accords, or in the serpentine conglomerate of commissions and teams specified to implement and police the provisions of the agreement.

A Two-Party Joint Military Commission (TPJMC) and a Four-Party Joint Military Commission (FPJMC) set forth in the accords and the protocols were immediately established as the entities to carry out the specific tasks which were to lead toward ending the war and restoring peace in Vietnam. The FPJMC included representatives from the United States, the Republic of Vietnam, the Democratic Republic of Vietnam (North Vietnam), and the Provisional Revolutionary Government (the Viet Cong), and was to exist for only 60 days. The TPJMC was to have a more enduring tenure, however. The TPJMC, that included only the two South Vietnamese factions, the RVN and the PRG, was charged to carry out the implementation of those articles of the Paris agreements which were viewed as strictly within the South Vietnamese purview, and which would supposedly lead toward national reconciliation. Examination of the history of the 60-day period following the signing of the Paris Accords reveals the frustrations, disappointments, failures, and successes achieved by those who toiled to implement these agreements.[3]

One of the most critical failures of the FPJMC was its inability to achieve a meaningful cease-fire, a failure which later would have a telling effect on US efforts to resolve the fate of still missing servicemen. This failure seemed to be pre-ordained because of the inherent RVN suspicion of the motives of the other two Vietnamese (communist) parties, and even more so because of the lack of resolve of any of the Vietnamese parties to make the accords work. The RVN signed the Paris Accords reluctantly in the first place, saw the agreement as having given the communists political and military advantage. Certainly the communist side saw the Paris Accords as but another means toward their goal of eventual reunification of North and South Vietnam under a communist government. The record of their delegations to these respective teams and commissions clearly bears out this perception of their goal. One telling example of the communists' attitude was the constant refusal by their delegates to participate in joint investigations of cease-fire violations as their troops continued to expand their control in the countryside.

On the plus side, however, was the successful disengagement of the remaining US forces from Vietnam and, equally important, the return of captured US military and civilian prisoners during Operation Homecoming—both events implemented during the 60-day life of the FPJMC. The depiction of these joyful events on television, after so many years of TV coverage of death and destruction, signified to much of the American populace the end of the war. In actuality, however, the fighting quickly began anew, this time without the participation of American forces, and with only a brief respite immediately following the signing of the Paris Accords.

THE FOUR-PARTY JOINT MILITARY TEAM

One of the protocols to the Paris Peace Accords made provision for a residual Four-Party Joint Military Team (FPJMT) to carry on the search and accounting for missing individuals following the 60-day termination of the

FPJMC activities. This team, with representation from the same four parties making up the Four-Party Joint Military Commission, came into existence in early 1973 and remained in place in Saigon until the eventual fall of the Government of the Republic of Vietnam on 30 April 1975. The US delegation to this FPJMT became, in essence, the US negotiating entity to deal with the DRV and the PRG in carrying out Article 8(b) of the Paris Accords.

The US delegation of the FPJMT was a group of less than twenty military personnel from all services, many with knowledge of unique value to the effort at hand. These included specialists in international law and history, individuals familiar with negotiation techniques, plus an array of interpreters, translators, and support personnel. The chief of the US delegation, (initially Colonel B. H. Russell, USA) represented the US position in matters pertaining to implementing Article 8(b). He received guidance from a number of sources, including both the Department of State, via Ambassador Ellsworth Bunker in Saigon, and the Department of Defense.

The FPJMT negotiations tested the patience of the US personnel, just as had the earlier negotiations in Paris. The two communist parties, the DRV and the PRG, continued to stall, using any pretext to avoid substantive discussion. Plenary meetings, scheduled twice weekly at Camp Davis on Tan Son Nhut Air Base in Saigon, were viewed by the DRV and PRG delegates as simply another forum in which to carry on the political battle to achieve what they had earlier been unable to attain at the conference table in Paris. DRV promises of assistance in resolving the fate of missing US personnel were usually made conditional on US willingness to urge our ally, the RVN, to make various, unacceptable concessions. At other times, the DRV and PRG would refuse to engage in discussion, alleging that the United States and the RVN were colluding to prolong the hostilities and violate the cease-fire, meanwhile ignoring the ongoing actions of their own troops who were busily engaged in nibbling away at what remained of RVN-held territory.

In this environment, efforts by the United States and RVN delegates to achieve substantive progress generally proved futile. Requests for information about specific cases of missing individuals remained totally unanswered. Information passed was received by the communist delegations without comment or response. US efforts to negotiate field investigation efforts in areas controlled by either the DRV or the PRG were met with delaying tactics, polemics, and inaction on the part of the communist delegations.

Attempts to get the communist DRV and PRG delegations to focus on implementation of Article 8(b) often resulted in introduction of various "red herring" issues designed to divert attention away from the task at hand. For example, the DRV at one point threatened to shoot down the USAF weekly C–130 liaison flight between Saigon and Hanoi after one such flight, on 21 December 1973, had allegedly "exceeded maneuvering limits" during a foul weather approach into Gia Lam Airport in Hanoi. This threat was taken seriously, even though DRV and PRG representatives were always aboard these liaison flights. The communists had already provided ample proof of their capability and willingness to carry out such threats, undeterred even by concern for their own personnel. On 7 April 1973 near Khe Sanh, the communists had shot down an official helicopter of the International Commission for Control and Supervision (ICCS) killing all eleven men aboard, including two PRG liaison officers.

At other points during the FPJMT talks the DRV and PRG representatives would make various demands concerning what they termed their "privileges and immunities," dwelling on their perceived poor treatment at the hands of their southern non-communist hosts in Saigon. In sum, the good intentions of the United States and RVN delegations to the FPJMT during the team's two year existence were generally thwarted by the intransigence and inaction of the DRV and PRG delegates. Consequently, little progress was achieved in carrying out the casualty resolution tasks specified in Article 8(b) of the Paris Accords.

The one notable positive event which transpired during the existence of the FPJMT was the repatriation from Hanoi of the remains of 23 American servicemen who had died while in captivity in the north.[4] Even this, however, was not accomplished without torment. Though the DRV had earlier provided a list during the final negotiations in Paris of those who had died while held in captivity, and had even permitted a visit to the grave sites near Hanoi by US delegates in May of 1973, the subsequent negotiations by the FPJMT for the return of these remains took nearly a year to accomplish.[5] These 23 remains were finally repatriated from Hanoi to United States custody in two increments on 6 and 13 March 1974. Indicative of the tenor of these negotiations was the refusal by the DRV to repatriate the remains of a twenty-fourth serviceman whose body had been buried alongside those of the other 23. The excuse was the technicality that he had died, not while in captivity, but as a consequence of being shot down.

Some have speculated, however, regarding a possible alternate rationale for the DRV refusal to return these remains. With the benefit of 20-20 hindsight, it became known that the "twenty-fourth remains" were those of B–52 aircrewman 1/Lt Bennie L. Fryer who had been shot down on 28 December 1972, just a few weeks prior to the cease-fire. Thus, at the time that the FPJMT discussions were taking place regarding the return of those others who had died while in captivity, it is perhaps understandable that the DRV may have been reluctant to disinter remains which had so recently been buried. To do so would be contrary to North Vietnamese health and sanitary concerns, as well as contrary to the usual Vietnamese practice in dealing with human remains which would normally call for the remains to be interred a minimum of two years prior to disinterment. Regardless of the rationale, the remains of 1/Lt Fryer were belatedly repatriated, more than four years later, on 30 September 1977.

It should be noted that the PRG also had provided a list in Paris of those they said had died while in captivity in South Vietnam. This list proved to be strange in several respects. It was alleged to include the names of all those who had died while in the custody of the communist PRG, and carried the names of 40 Americans and 7 foreign nationals. The list contained several explainable anomalies (misspelled names, wrong nationality, wrong military status, etc.), but also included three more significant errors which prompted considerable amount of discussion and speculation on the part of US negotiators. PFC James J. Scuitier and Sgt Billy Knight, whose names were on the list, had indeed been killed in Vietnam. However, their remains were immediately recovered by US forces at the time of their respective incidents, were positively identified, and promptly returned to the United States for burial. At no time were their remains ever in the hands of Viet Cong (PRG) troops. Even more curious was the presence on the list of the name Carl Nicotera. Nicotera had served in Vietnam, but was discharged from the US Army in October 1968 and at last word was living in Hartford, Connecticut. How Nicotera's name found its way onto the PRG died-in-captivity list remains an unsolved mystery. The discrepancies of the PRG list notwithstanding, US attempts through the auspices of the FPJMT to gain the release of any of these remains, or to obtain any additional information regarding these individuals, were totally without result.

JOINT CASUALTY RESOLUTION CENTER

While the FPJMT constituted the negotiating element of the US effort, another entity, the Joint Casualty Resolution Center (JCRC), was created as the operational element. The JCRC was a unique organization in the annals of military history. Activated in Saigon on 23 January 1973, its first Commander was Brigadier General Robert C. Kingston, a hard-driving infantry officer with considerable background experience in special operations.[6] The JCRC mission was solely to assist the Secretaries of the Armed Services to resolve the fate of those servicemen still missing and unaccounted for as a result of the hostilities throughout Indochina. The unit was to have a predominantly operational role—the carrying out of field search, excavation, recovery, and repatriation activities negotiated through the FPJMT.[7]

General Kingston gathered the initial JCRC cadre in Saigon, calling for volunteers and drawing heavily from among military personnel still remaining in-country at that time (January 1973). He personally interviewed each volunteer, accepting those whose talents matched a menu of personnel skills previously drawn up by the military planners at CINCPAC in Hawaii as the Paris negotiations were wending their way toward conclusion.[8] The personnel roster, with an initial authorization for approximately 140 persons, was heavily loaded on the side of field search teams. These teams were almost entirely composed of Army Special Forces personnel; however, in keeping with the joint nature of the organization, members of all four military services were represented within the unit. In addition to the search teams, the JCRC also included a sizeable staff element to refine, analyze, update, and store the records pertaining to each of the casualty cases. While the personnel authorization for the JCRC underwent several revisions and peaked out at nearly 200 positions, the assigned strength of the unit grew to a maximum of only 160 persons by mid-1973.

The JCRC case records were inherited from another little-known military unit in Vietnam which was named the Joint Personnel Recovery Center (JPRC).[9] The JPRC, which had already been operational in Vietnam for over six years, had the mission of attempting to rescue American prisoners-of-war and, consequently, had collected considerable information and had generated numerous files on those individuals who had disappeared. Therefore, with the establishment of the Joint Casualty Resolution Center, the old JPRC files constituted a logical starting point for the entire casualty resolution effort that was to follow. Efforts were soon launched by the JCRC to expand and update these files, beginning immediately with the debriefing of all POWs released during Operation Homecoming in February and March of 1973.

Though the JCRC was activated in Vietnam, because of the US interpretation of the restrictions imposed by the Paris Accords on the number of US military personnel who could be left in Vietnam, the unit was immediately moved to Nakhon Phanom Air Base in northeast Thailand. Here the JCRC Headquarters was established, the personnel and files were assembled, and training programs were begun in anticipation of the start of search, exhumation, and repatriation activities back in Vietnam. Close liaison was established back in Saigon with the FPJMT which was to negotiate the access to various aircraft crash sites and ground loss sites. In addition, a formal relationship was established between the JCRC and the US Army Central Identification Laboratory which had recently moved from Saigon to Camp Samae San, also in Thailand. This laboratory, staffed with both military and civilian experts, was to examine and identify any remains which might be recovered as a result of either JCRC search efforts, or any unilateral repatriations of remains by Vietnamese members of the FPJMT.

To further enhance the effectiveness of the JCRC organization US plans called for the establishment of several small JCRC liaison offices to be located in each of the countries of interest. Consequently, in early 1973 a small contingent of military personnel were relocated in Saigon to constitute what was to be called the Saigon Liaison Office of the JCRC. At the same time another small office, to be known as the Hanoi Liaison Office, was also placed in Saigon in hopeful anticipation of its movement from Saigon to Hanoi whenever the FPJMT could negotiate such a transfer. As previously mentioned, a spirit of cooperation was lacking in our relations with the North Vietnamese delegation to the FPJMT. As a result, the Hanoi Liaison Office was never repositioned to Hanoi and it was subsequently folded into the Saigon

Liaison Office a few months before the collapse of South
Vietnam in early 1975.

In Vientiane, Laos, one man was sent to work in the
American Embassy as the JCRC Liaison Officer, though
his effectiveness was extremely limited by the political
turmoil and the American embassy's inability to deal seriously with the communist Pathet Lao regarding missing
Americans. This office, too, was closed when the communists took over the government of Laos in mid-1975. In
Cambodia, also, the chaotic situation prevented the
JCRC Commander from obtaining agreement to place
any JCRC liaison personnel in Phnom Penh to deal with
American losses in Khmer territory.

JCRC OPERATIONS BEGIN

The men and women of the newly-formed JCRC,
sensing the 'uniqueness' of their mission and filled with
a sense of high endeavor, were eager to begin the task of
attempting to recover the remains of their fallen comrades-in-arms. Based on a review of loss records and the
examination of numerous other factors, several candidate
sites were selected for possible JCRC exploration in early
1973. One of the prime selection criterian was security of
the area. Since the communist FPJMT delegates refused
to grant approval for search activities within territory
which they claimed was under their control, sites were
selected which were believed to be well within the control
area of our ally, the RVN. After coordination and approval by the American embassy in Saigon, the United
States delegate tabled the planned JCRC activities before
the FPJMT, and invitations to witness the activity were
extended to all delegations. In every instance, however,
the DRV and PRG delegates refused to discuss these
operations, noting only that the FPJMT had not approved the investigations. Nevertheless, the US delegate
continued to notify all FPJMT members whenever any
JCRC activities were planned.

Once the proposed search and recovery activities were coordinated with the American embassy in Saigon and approved by the RVN, the JCRC teams were flown from Thailand to Saigon, and thence to a staging area near the search locale. These teams customarily included such specialists as crashsite investigators, graves registration experts, medics, explosive ordnance disposal technicians, and interpreters. Teams and their equipment were commonly moved to the vicinity of the search area via trucks. However, various means of transport were used, including backpacking. In one instance, because of the remoteness and ruggedness of the area, they were forced to rappel into a Khanh Hoa Province crashsite from CH–53 helicopters hovering above the dense jungle canopy.

The JCRC acknowledged that assistance from the local populace could be helpful, not only as laborers during excavations, but also in determining the exact location of aircraft crashsites and suspected US grave sites. In several instances the information provided by local inhabitants was key to locating American remains. One such effort occurred in May of 1973 when a JCRC team attempted to locate the grave site of an American aviator who was shot by the Viet Cong after successfully crash-landing his observation aircraft on a beach near Tuy Hoa. A three-day digging effort resulted in the movement of an estimated 100 tons of sand, but proved fruitless until a local fisherman came forward to pinpoint the exact grave location based on his personal recollection of the burial years earlier.

During its first ten months of activity, JCRC teams participated in over a dozen search and recovery activities throughout South Vietnam. The result of this effort was the recovery of the remains of 21 individuals, eleven of which were identified as those of Americans. Of the remainder, five were indeterminate and five were proven to be those of ''Southeast Asian Mongoloids'' (Vietnamese); these latter were to be eventually repatriated by the Central Identification Laboratory back to Vietnamese authorities.[10]

SEA SALVAGE OPERATIONS

Of the approximately 2,500 individuals unaccounted for at the end of active US involvement in the fighting in early 1973, over 400 had been categorized as "over-water" losses. This meant that these individuals were believed to have been lost at sea, either as a result of having crashed into the water, or as a result of drowning after an untoward incident—being washed overboard from a ship, for example. No one had any illusions regarding the ultimate fate of those listed in this category; however, because of the number involved the JCRC Commander ordered that an attempt should be made to determine the likelihood of recovering any identifiable remains.

To answer this question, the US Navy Supervisor of Salvage was asked to design and conduct an off-shore search and recovery program under JCRC direction. After a data analysis was completed, a search locale was selected off the Vietnam coast in the region between the cities of Danang and Hué. This coastal sea area was the scene of a relatively high number of aircraft crashsites, and was thought to afford the maximum opportunity to test the concept of underwater location and recovery of remains. The actual search effort (nicknamed SEASAL) began on 10 July 1973, with the US Navy bringing to this task the latest undersea technology. The search concept included location of aircraft wreckage on the sea bottom by a sophisticated side-looking sonar scanner operated from an instrumented barge. From this barge, which could be precisely placed and anchored, divers would descend to the bottom to physically investigate any aircraft wreckage which was located. As one search area was completely surveyed, the barge was moved to the next area. By 15 August a stretch of coastal waters covering 48 square miles of ocean bottom had been systematically searched, and numerous wrecks of crashed aircraft were individually investigated.

The results of this effort were disappointing but not unexpected. The often-imagined scene of the World War II aircraft sitting relatively intact on the ocean floor had no parallel in the case of the average modern jet fighter. The divers' inspections confirmed that these aircraft, due primarily to their speed, had disintegrated to nearly the same extent as if they had crashed on land. Wings and control surfaces were ripped off, engines were broken from fuselages, and—worst of all—cockpits were shattered and torn asunder. This initial crash trauma, the time lapse since the event, and the effect of seawater immersion combined to preclude the successful recovery of identifiable remains. By the time the SEASAL effort was officially halted on 29 September 1973, 82 days had elapsed, the activity had cost $830,000, and only a few bone fragments, unidentifiable, had been recovered from one crash site.[11] Based on these results, the JCRC Commander made the strong recommendation that no further at-sea casualty resolution operations be conducted.

Over the past decade the remains of several aviators who were classified as "over-water" losses have been returned by Vietnamese officials. Later analysis has shown, however, that these were the remains of fliers whose bodies were recovered from the water by fishermen, taken ashore, and interred. One other additional hope, relatively remote, for recovery of the remains of individuals classed as "over-water" losses, are cases where the "over-water" classification was made in error. (In a number of cases the loss location is not precisely known, being based on such indefinite information as planned flight track or radio contacts and may be at best an educated guess.[12]) These exceptions aside, and in view of the empirical evidence gathered from the JCRC sponsored SEASAL recovery effort, it seems the lesson to be learned is that it is unrealistic to expect that more than a few of the "over-water" cases will ever be resolved by the recovery of identifiable remains.

"PUBLIC COMMUNICATIONS" AND THE REWARDS PROGRAM

The original planning for the JCRC envisioned an effort to solicit casualty related information from the

indigenous population. In many instances US case records were lacking in vital details regarding what occurred during the loss incident. It was the JCRC view that
knowledgeable individuals could be enticed to come forward and assist, either by providing firsthand knowledge
or by referring investigators to others who had such information. An offer of rewards for information and/or assistance was planned to aid in this "enticement".
Consequently, a program was formulated whereby various media would be used to inform the general populace
of the US casualty resolution effort, and solicit their assistance in providing pertinent information.

Implementation of this "public communication"
(PUBCOM) program proved to be a slow process. Expertise and personnel were quickly obtained through the
Army's 7th PSYOP Group in Okinawa to formulate the
specific media messages to be used. These personnel, including 5 native Vietnamese specialists, joined the JCRC
headquarters in Thailand and became known as the Media Development Element (MDE). Within a short period
of time, information pamphlets were prepared, in Vietnamese, to advise key communicators—governmental officials, clergy, military officials—of the American
casualty resolution effort. In addition, work began on
radio scripts, posters, and other handout materials to dis-
seminate on a much wider basis details about the JCRC,
its activities, and its desire for information about US casualties.

Problems arose when the JCRC attempted to obtain
permission, through the American embassy in Saigon,
for release and distribution of these items. The embassy
had assumed an extremely cautious position regarding
the entire JCRC effort. On the one hand was the requirement to get on with the casualty resolution effort as an
important humanitarian matter; on the other hand was
the need to refrain from doing anything which might scut-
tle the discussions going on among the members of the
FPJMT and which, hopefully, would lead to the greater
gain. Consequently, the American embassy in Saigon
voiced strong reservations when the controversial topic of

rewards came up for intensive review in mid-1973. Rewards for indigenous assistance had been an integral part of the information-collection effort of the Joint Personnel Recovery Center, and CINCPAC had dictated that a reward program would also be a part of the JCRC effort. The ambassador in Saigon, however, doubted the advisability of publicizing such a program. The embassy view was that the communist parties to the Paris Accords would take offense at such a program, and the embassy did not wish to provide the communists with any excuse to escape their obligation to properly implement these agreements.

Before this issue could be properly resolved, however, the topic of rewards surfaced in early June 1973 in the Saigon press when three different local newspapers announced that the United States was offering "money, bicycles, and agricultural tools" as incentives for the local populace to come forward with information regarding the remains of American soldiers. In a masterful bit of bad timing, the next day a *Stars and Stripes* story quoted the CINCPAC, Admiral Noel Gayler, saying in a San Diego speech that the United States would provide "considerable rewards to people in remote areas" for their assistance to the casualty resolution effort.[13] In a damage limitation effort, CINCPAC quickly clarified that no rewards would be paid unless JCRC personnel were on-site to confirm the information provided, that no rewards for remains would be paid unless and until the remains were positively identified as those of missing American personnel, and that a schedule of rewards would be promulgated by the JCRC. This schedule, released within several days, offered the following:

- $50-$75 for directing a team to another individual who has casualty resolution information.

- $75-$100 for information leading to the recovery of the remains of a missing American.

- $100-$150 for guiding JCRC personnel to a crashsite or gravesite.

A poster on a tree in Can Tho City solicits casualty resolution information from the local populace.

• The above rewards may be paid in material goods rather than US currency.

On 14 June 1973, responding to the publicity surrounding the announcement of payment of rewards, the DRV delegate to the FPJMT expressed his indignation over the rewards program, saying that it "distorted the humanitarian policy of the DRV" regarding compliance with Article 8(b) of the Paris Accords. Ambassador Ellsworth Bunker in Saigon, while not taking issue with the existence of a rewards program, again reiterating his request that the program not be further publicized.

The strain resulting from the controversial reward issue seemed to carry over into the implementation of the overall public communications program. Consequently, when presented with the idea of displaying posters country-wide, broadcasting radio "spots," or of distributing free wall and pocket calendars among the populace (the calendars also carried a message soliciting casualty resolution information), the embassy balked. JCRC persistence in promoting the PUBCOM program, though it heightened the perception of strains between it and the American embassy, was belatedly successful. After undertaking a lengthy review of the program, soliciting comments from the US Information Service and the four regional consuls general, and assessing the extent of progress in the FPJMT talks, the ambassador finally agreed on 12 March 1974 to permit a country-wide public communication program on a phased basis. This program began on 18 March 1974, and was fully implemented country-wide by mid-June. Thereafter, adding new media elements came easier, but this did not allay the belief on the part of some that the year's delay in actively soliciting information from the general Vietnamese populace had resulted in casualty resolution opportunities lost.

MORE CASUALTIES AND A CHANGED CONCEPT

The US delegation to the FPJMT had, on a number of occasions, attempted to gain approval for field operations aimed at searching crashsites or gravesites in areas which were acknowledged to be under the control of the PRG. These attempts were met, first with delaying replies from the communists, and later with outright rejection of requests. Consequently, as mentioned earlier, the JCRC teams had to be content with working in areas which were deemed to be under the control of the RVN, our ally. Even in these instances, the PRG and DRV had voiced their objections over the JCRC activities, usually by contending that the area to be searched was, in fact, within an area which was under their control. Since there was no clear delineation of these areas, such claims were always a matter of concern when planning any search and recovery operations.

Because of the communist delegates' attitude, coupled with the resurgence in the fighting following the brief lull of the January 1973 cease-fire, everyone perceived the inherent danger associated with field operations. Concerted attempts were made to minimize this danger by means of careful planning and preparation. Intelligence estimates were made in coordination with our RVN ally, the American embassy, and other available intelligence assets. Only if everyone agreed that the degree of risk was minimal would the American Embassy approve the initiation of any search or recovery activity. It was acknowledged that the field teams were essentially defenseless in the event of attack since they were, by agreement, unarmed. Thus, to assure recognition as part of the organizational apparatus set up by the Paris Accords, teams travelled in helicopters marked with four wide orange stripes which surrounded the fuselage, and team members wore uniforms which were prominently marked with bright orange pockets. One last mark of identity was the bright orange armband worn by each team member signifying his association with the FPJMT.

By the end of 1973 a number of JCRC field operations had been conducted with no security problems. The US delegation to the FPJMT had routinely notified all other delegates of the on-going US casualty resolution operations, and even invited each delegation, including the PRG and the DRV, to send representatives to witness these activities. The two communist delegations made note of these field activities but consistently declined the opportunity to send any observers.

In early December 1973, another JCRC field activity began. The site of interest, a helicopter crashsite, was located approximately 20 kilometers southwest of Saigon in an area of rice and pineapple fields, low trees, and brush. The rice fields, abandoned for a number of years, had grown up with tall grass and weeds but were still flooded with knee-deep water and mud. Captain Richard Rees, the JCRC field team leader on this operation, flew with his team and equipment to the crash site aboard FPJMT-marked helicopters on the morning of 13 December. Work was immediately begun to construct a mud dike which would surround the crash impact point and the minimal amount of helicopter wreckage which still remained at the site. Rees' plan was to construct the circular dike, then pump the water from inside the dike to the outside, thereby drying the area to permit a thorough search for the remains of the long-lost crewman who disappeared when the helicopter had crashed over seven years earlier.[14] By the end of the second day, the circular dike was nearly completed.

On the morning of the third day, 15 December, Rees and his team again boarded the FPJMT helicopters at Tan Son Nhut airport in Saigon for the short 15-minute flight back to the crashsite. This time they had with them portable water pumps with which they hoped to pump dry the area surrounding the wreckage. The three helicopters circled to land, intending to rest their skids gently on the paddy dikes so that the heavy pumps could then be unloaded from the helicopters. The first of the three helicopters hovered down to a landing. Touching down gently, Rees and his men hopped out as the Vietnamese pilot held the craft stable on the dike. The other two helicopters commenced their landing adjacent to the first. Suddenly a communist B–40 rocket-propelled grenade exploded against the first helicopter, setting it afire and fatally wounding one of the Vietnamese crewmen. Though hit by shrapnel, the other two helicopters immediately took to the air to escape a similar fate. With their means of escape gone, Captain Rees and his unarmed team were at the mercy of the automatic weapons fire which the Viet Cong ambushers now raked across the paddy field.

Rees and his men threw themselves down into the knee-deep water, hoping that the weeds and old paddy dikes would provide some degree of cover from the ambushers' fire. Captain Rees quickly realized that they were totally at the mercy of their attackers, and that no help could be expected from either of the unarmed helicopters which were now circling overhead. In a final courageous gamble to save his team, Rees stood up with his hands raised, and shouted in Vietnamese to the attackers to stop their firing because his men were unarmed. His shout was immediately answered by a volley of fire from the brush at the edge of the paddy, and Captain Rees fell dead into the water.

One can only speculate why the ambushers did not pursue the attack to completion. Perhaps it was their uncertainty of whether or not the circling helicopters, which made zooming passes overhead, were armed or not. Perhaps they expected a relief force to arrive shortly to assist the pinned-down Americans lying helpless in the rice paddy. Or perhaps they had made their point and had sufficiently carried out the orders of their PRG superiors. Whatever the reason, the Viet Cong quickly withdrew from the scene leaving behind one American killed and four team members wounded, one Vietnamese killed and three wounded, and one helicopter destroyed.

The events that followed were totally predictable. At the next plenary session of the FPJMT, Colonel William Tombaugh, then chief of the US delegation, delivered a blistering attack on the PRG and their DRV ally. He accused them of treachery in using information provided by the United States during the FPJMT talks to deliberately engineer the coordinated ambush of an unarmed team clearly marked with the Four-Party markings and carrying out the humanitarian work of the FPJMT. The PRG representative denied any complicity in the event, protested the "hostile attitude" of Colonel Tombaugh

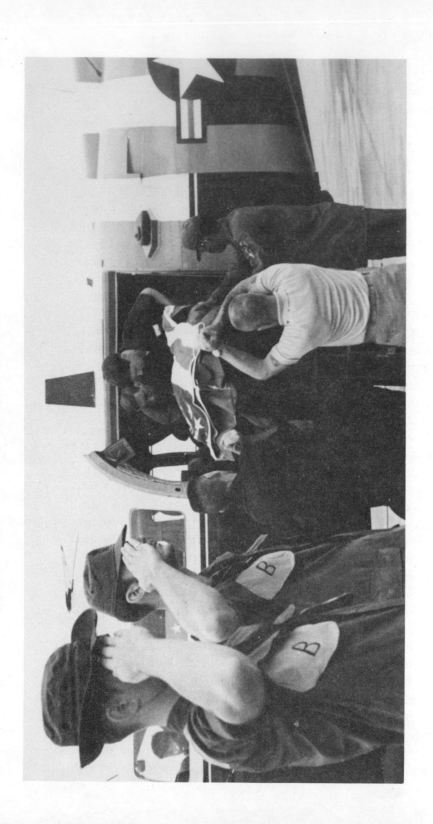

JCRC members load the flag-covered body of Captain Richard Rees onto an aircraft in Saigon. Captain Rees was killed in an ambush earlier in the day while leading a team on a casualty resolution operation.

(who, in the course of his attack on the PRG, had thrown Rees' blood-soaked shirt onto the table in front of the startled PRG delegate), and demanded that the United States desist from "falsely accusing" them of perpetrating the fatal ambush. Meanwhile, in the United States there was only brief press mention of the incident. Captain Rees' killers had correctly judged the shift in media attention, and along with it the degree of public apathy regarding events in Vietnam once the American forces had been withdrawn.

The significance of the PRG ambush of an unarmed JCRC field team went well beyond the tragedy of the loss of life and wounding of the Americans and Vietnamese directly involved. Here was clear evidence of the intransigence of the communist parties to the Paris Accords, clear indications of the lengths to which they would go to sabotage these agreements, and a vivid preview of their unwillingness to cooperate in what should have been viewed as a solely humanitarian endeavor—the recovery of the remains of soldiers—from all sides—and the return of these remains to their families. It was now all too obvious that the DRV and PRG did not share these high-minded goals.

The JCRC Commander, now BG Joseph Ulatoski, was faced with either giving up the effort, or creating a new concept which might permit continuation of the mission. It was obvious that inserting unarmed American search and recovery teams into the field was no longer feasible. Thus, after a number of consultations among the JCRC, the American embassy, and our South Vietnamese allies, a scheme was devised whereby the JCRC would train and equip South Vietnamese Army troops to carry on the search and recovery activity. US guidance, planning, and technical assistance would be provided from a safe location, away from the actual field search and recovery site.

The necessary actions were undertaken to immediately implement this new concept, and casualty resolution activity once again resumed in early 1974, with the actual location and exhumation of remains being carried out by

South Vietnamese soldiers. Under the new guidelines from the American embassy, only in those rare instances where complete safety could be assured were JCRC members permitted to take part in the search and recovery activity.[15] In all other instances, JCRC personnel were obliged to participate only from a distance, and to assume nothing more than an advisory role in their relations with the indigenous team in the field. In this manner, and under increasingly difficult circumstances, the JCRC continued their casualty resolution efforts during 1974. By August, the US-trained indigenous teams had participated in 15 investigation and remains recovery activities, with 36 remains recovered, of which 5 had been identified as those of United States personnel.

A REDUCED JCRC

Meanwhile, due to the disappointing results, the declining military situation throughout the countryside, poor access to sites of interest, and the lack of progress in the FPJMT sessions, CINCPAC directed a review, in mid-1974, of the JCRC mission and organization. Recommendations included continued emphasis on the use of indigenous teams to carry out field investigations and remains recoveries. At the same time, any US teams brought into Vietnam were to be smaller in size to reduce the physical risk and to lower their political profile. Emphasis was placed on refining the JCRC data files to increase their accuracy, and to continue the exchange of data with the US delegation of the FPJMT in support of their on-going negotiations with the DRV and PRG. The JCRC was also to continue its analysis of case files in order to make recommendations regarding status changes (from MIA to KIA) to the various military services. Additionally, CINCPAC made other recommendations regarding the staffing of the JCRC, to include reduction of the number of JCRC field teams from 11 to four, a corresponding reduction in JCRC staff members, reduction of the rank of the JCRC Commander's billet from Brigadier General to Colonel, and physical movement of the JCRC organization from Nakhon Phanom Air Base to Camp Samae San in southeast Thailand.

The Joint Chiefs of Staff (JCS) in Washington DC received these recommendations but, aware of the political sensitivities involved, concluded that making any sweeping organizational changes at this time would be premature. The JCS did not wish to take any action which might be interpreted as decreasing the emphasis of the casualty resolution effort, or of abandoning the JCRC mission. They did, however, approve the movement of the JCRC to Samae San, since military activities at Nakhon Phanom Air Base were gradually being closed down. This move eventually took place in January 1975.

Meanwhile, the military situation throughout Indochina continued to deteriorate. The FPJMT talks were essentially stalemated, and the DRV and PRG representatives no longer made any pretense of pursuing efforts to carry out either the terms of Article 8(b), or of any other portion of the Paris Accords, including those dealing with the cessation of hostilities. Like a big deadly chess game, the North Vietnamese relentlessly pushed their men into place for the final checkmate. By the end of 1974, an estimated 300,000 North Vietnamese Army troops were in South Vietnam, an increase of over 90,000 since the date of the cease-fire. In addition, these troops were supported by an increasing number of tanks, heavy artillery, and Surface-to-Air (SAM) missiles. The North Vietnamese had constructed and improved over 1,000 miles of roadways to facilitate their infiltration of men and supplies into the south, and had turned the city of Dong Ha into a major port and stockpile site.[16] Hope for the successful conclusion of any meaningful effort to resolve the American casualties lost in South Vietnam was rapidly fading.

As this deterioration continued into the first months of 1975, the JCRC effort in Vietnam ground to a halt. The public communication program ceased, as did other attempts to solicit assistance from officials and community leaders. Planning for site investigations was put on hold, and the JCRC headquarters in Thailand devoted itself more and more to analytical efforts. Our South Vietnamese allies, preoccupied as they were with their own survival, could no longer devote any energy or resources to assisting the United States in resolving the fate of American casualties.

By March 1975, all offensive momentum had turned in favor of the communist forces. Much of the Central Highlands had fallen or was under siege, and the northern provinces of South Vietnam were falling in turn. The North Vietnamese war machine ground its way southward, pushing ahead of it a wave of panic designed to break the resistance of Saigon. All United States efforts at casualty resolution in South Vietnam had necessarily ceased, and the JCRC liaison personnel were co-opted by the American Defense Attaché in Saigon to assist in responding to the approaching debacle. Several personnel were detailed to assist with the humanitarian aspects of the flood of Vietnamese refugees who were pouring into the Saigon area from up-country areas which the communist forces had already overrun. Other JCRC personnel were assigned to assist in preparing for the evacuation of both American and Vietnamese personnel.

In the midst of this frantic activity, in early April a USAF C–5 aircraft crashed at Tan Son Nhut Air Base near Saigon killing many of the passengers and crew aboard, including over 100 Vietnamese orphans who were being evacuated to the United States. The Defense Attaché, taking advantage of the availability and expertise of the JCRC and the Army's Central Identification Laboratory, directed that they assume responsibility for the recovery and disposition of the bodies of those killed in the crash. Thus the JCRC and Central Identification Laboratory personnel conducted their last and saddest casualty operation in South Vietnam prior to the final evacuation.

On 21 April, the JCRC Commander Colonel John P. Vollmer, directed that the remaining JCRC personnel still in Vietnam be evacuated. Colonel Vollmer had several overriding concerns, the first being the immediate safety of his personnel. Second, however, was his concern that should JCRC personnel remain in Vietnam to the last, they would ultimately become involved in the renewed conflict, thus distorting the image of the JCRC which he and previous commanders had sought to maintain: that the JCRC was strictly a humanitarian organization, overt in all its activities, and not to be involved in combat of any form. An Army U–21 aircraft was dispatched from Thailand, and the last of the JCRC liaison office personnel were loaded aboard. The plane returned across Cambodia to Thailand where the liaison office members rejoined the JCRC headquarters at Camp Samae San.[17]

The complete collapse of our South Vietnamese ally came nine days later as the North Vietnamese Army tanks rolled into Saigon on the morning of April 30. Earlier that same morning the last of the official American presence in Saigon had departed from the American embassy rooftop helicopter pad, including the ambassador and the remaining members of the US delegation to the FPJMT. At the same time, the American consul general in Can Tho had led the only other remaining official American contingent in an escape by boat down the Mekong River and out into the South China Sea where they were later picked up by US Navy ships.

Only a few hours before, the last two American casualties in Vietnam were incurred when an in-coming rocket killed two young Marines who were assisting with the Saigon evacuation. In a twist of regrettable irony, during the chaos of those final hours their remains were left behind in a Saigon hospital, not to be recovered and returned to their homeland until nearly a year later.[18]

NOTES

1. Henry Kissinger, *White House Years* (Boston: Little, Brown & Co., 1979), chaps.8, 12, 23, 25, 27, 31-34 passim. Kissinger provides a most interesting and detailed account of the negotiations in Paris. The Paris plenary sessions, according to Kissinger, as contrasted with the direct talks between himself and North Vietnamese officials, "achieved a great distinction in the annals of diplomacy. In four years of negotiation and more than 140 meetings not even the most minor issue had been settled; it was the only regular conference of such length that could not point to a single accomplishment, however trivial." p. 1106.

2. Ibid., pp. 441-2, 975. Kissinger describes at some length the Vietnamese negotiation style, a style which he several times refers to as an extreme test of his sanity. US personnel later involved in attempts to resolve the issue of unaccounted for Americans were to encounter the same maddening techniques in the course of their dealings with Hanoi counterparts.

3. Walter Scott Dillard, *Sixty Days to Peace* (Washington, DC: National Defense University Press, 1982). Colonel Dillard, a historian by academic training and profession, provides a well-documented and very interesting account of the 60-day life of the Four-Party Joint Military Commission, of which he was a member.

4. It is a known fact that more than 23 men died while in captivity in North Vietnam. The semantic ruse which the DRV later used to justify listing only 23, however, was to claim that the others "weren't in captivity when they died". The DRV apparently defined "captivity" as including only those incarcerated in the "formal" POW prison system at the national level, therefore excluding those who died while in the hands of the local populace or the militia, while in local prisons, or while en route to detention in this so-called "formal" prison system.

5. Among the sticking points during the negotiations for the return of these remains was the DRV insistence on linking this repatriation to their demand that all parties agree and sign a document outlining the "modalities and general principles" for implementing Article 8(b). Later, in another delaying tactic, the DRV linked their cooperation to the return of civilian

(communist) detainees still allegedly being held by the government of the RVN, a linkage which the United States had steadfastly rejected. Other similar tactics were also later used to delay the return of the died-in-captivity (DIC) remains.

6. Before his eventual retirement from the Army in 1985, General Kingston attained four-star rank as the Commander in Chief of the United States Central Command in Tampa, Florida. He was later to reenter the arena of the MIA issue, when he became a member of General Vessey's delegation to Hanoi in August 1987, and again in later Vessey trips to Vietnam.

7. The mission of the JCRC, as described in JCS message 241751Z JAN 73, was to "resolve the status of United States missing/body not recovered personnel through the conduct of operations to locate and investigate crash/grave sites and recover remains, as appropriate, throughout southeast Asia as directed by COMUSSAG/7AF". (COMUSSAG/7AF was the Commander, United States Support Activities Group/7th Air Force, whose headquarters was located at Nakhon Phanom Air Base, Thailand.)

8. The formation of the JCRC was set forth in a conceptual plan drafted by the CINCPAC staff. This plan, CINCPAC CONPLAN 5119, was originally complemented by another plan, CINCPAC CONPLAN 5100, which dealt with the topic of the recovery of live personnel. By 1974, DOD realized that the return of live personnel, if any existed, would more likely take place via diplomatic effort rather than by military action, and in any event would be planned and coordinated at the Washington DC level instead of by CINCPAC. So, realizing that CINCPAC CONPLAN 5100 was unrealistic, JCS authorized, on 27 November 1974, the cancellation of this plan.

9. "Joint Personnel Recovery in SEA (U)", *Contemporary Historical Examination of Current Operations* (CHECO) Report CHECOD 75-0028, 5 February 1975, 7th Air Force. The Joint Personnel Recovery Center (JPRC) was activated on 17 September 1966 as an integral part of the MACV Studies and Observations Group (SOG) in Vietnam. Its mission was to pursue the long-term task of recovering US personnel after search and rescue (SAR) operations had been suspended. The JPRC served as the coordinating agency for the recovery of personnel who managed to evade capture, to escape, or those

who were occasionally released from captivity by the enemy. The JPRC was subsumed into the newly activated JCRC on 23 January 1973.

10. *CINCPAC Command History*, 1973 (TS), vol. I, 30 August 1974, p. 224.

11. Ibid., p. 222.

12. One such case of erroneous classification as an "over-water" loss was that of US Army Major George Quamo. He was a passenger aboard a Vietnamese aircraft which disappeared from radar view during inclement weather many miles off the coast of Danang on 14 April 1968. Though presumed to have been lost at sea, the wreckage of his aircraft was discovered in 1974 on a coastal ridge, in heavy jungle, and Major Quamo's remains were recovered.

13. *CINCPAC Command History*, 1973 (TS), vol. I, 30 August 1974, p. 175.

14. The unlocated crewman was Cpl David A. Dillon, who was aboard a UH-1B helicopter which crashed on 20 July 1966. However, Cpl Dillons' remains have never been recovered.

15. A search and recovery activity was undertaken in a school yard within the limits of the city of Hué in northern South Vietnam in August of 1974. In this instance the locale was deemed by the American embassy to be safe enough to permit US participation in the recovery effort. Coincidentally, the effort resulted in the successful recovery of the remains of a US government civilian official who had been killed during the 1968 Tet offensive in Hué city.

16. *CINCPAC Command History*, 1974 (TS), vol. I, p. 172, and vol. II, p. 544.

17. Two JCRC personnel, Captain George Petrie and Captain Tony Wood, remained in Saigon to the last. During the weeks before the collapse, they had been given vital roles in the planning and implementing of the final ground and helicopter evacuation from selected sites throughout Saigon. Consequently, in a paperwork ruse to maintain JCRC's non-combat image, Petrie and Wood were administratively separated from the JCRC and assigned to the Defense Attaché Office. Their heroic activities during this period would make a book in itself. So also would the activity of another JCRC member, Captain Roger Urbaniak, who was evacuated from Saigon to Thailand

on 21 April, signed out on leave, then, unbeknownst to the JCRC Commander, returned aboard an aircraft back to Saigon two days later to assist in the evacuation of the JCRC Liaison Office Vietnamese staff members.

18. The two Marines killed on 29 April 1975 during the US evacuation from Saigon were Lance Corporal Darwin L. Judge from Iowa and Corporal Charles McMahon, Jr. from Massachusetts. Immediately following their deaths, their remains were moved to the Seventh Day Adventist Hospital in Saigon. Upon completion of the final evacuation of official Americans the following morning, it was discovered that these two bodies had been overlooked in the chaos and had been left behind. The North Vietnamese victors discovered the remains in the hospital mortuary, and interred them in the Chi Hoa cemetery in Saigon. Finally, at the behest of Senator Edward Kennedy, on 22 February 1976 the DRV repatriated the remains of Judge and McMahon to the custody of two of Kennedy's staff members, Mr. Tinker and Mr. Dehaan, who then escorted the remains from Saigon to the Central Identification Laboratory in Thailand.

2

A WINDING DOWN

A PERIOD OF MALAISE

The fall of Saigon, preceded immediately by the fall of Phnom Penh and followed shortly by the takeover of Laos by the communist Pathet Lao, left the future of the American casualty resolution issue in great doubt. It almost seemed that the American public, in spite of the implications of these events, breathed a collective sigh of relief, and was prepared to put the whole Vietnam affair completely out of mind. Though there were high level administration statements in support of the casualty resolution mission and a show of congressional interest, the government also appeared to be entering a period of paralysis on the issue, and there was little indication of strong advocacy to continue the effort.

As expected, the exception was to be found among the families of those still unaccounted for. Their expectations were undiminished, their hopes unsatisfied, and their criticism of the US government over sparse concrete results to date was not muted.[1] No one in government, of course, dared speak out in open opposition to a continuation of effort; to do so would be political suicide. But within the Joint Casualty Resolution Center (JCRC), an organization whose sole reason for existence was the casualty resolution task, a sense of frustration arose from the realization that this issue now had—at best—only the divided attention of all other US governmental entities. Indeed, at times it seemed that the casualty resolution mission was fated to be damned by faint enthusiasm.

Even within the JCRC there were problems. Many dedicated individuals who had been working diligently on the casualty resolution mission were eager for a resumption of the effort, despite the dramatically changed circumstances. Some even went so far as to advocate early renewal of contact with the victorious DRV and PRG to get the effort back on track, a suggestion which was met with horror by a few less imaginative members of the unit. Understandably, for a very few individuals, residual bitterness over the outcome of the recent conflict held sway over the necessity to get on with the assigned mission.

The suggestion for early renewed contact with the DRV had not been made lightly, however. The DRV had asked quite emphatically in April 1975 that the United States delegation to the FPJMT stay on in Vietnam to continue discussions, even as North Vietnamese troops were pressing at the Saigon city limits. Further, by August 1975, the DRV and PRG were publicly stating their desire to reestablish contact with the United States, to include discussions on the fate of American MIAs.

Another problem for the JCRC was the reluctance to acknowledge that success in resolving the issue of American casualties would not be immediate, and only a long-term effort could yield any positive results. It was difficult, however, to instill such a long-term viewpoint when the military system dictated that unit assignments were to be only one year in length. The natural tendency was for assigned personnel to aim for the maximum short-term progress, or "results," during their one-year tour, then to move on to a new and hopefully more productive assignment. Thus, lack of personnel continuity had sometimes had negative results in the way the JCRC went about its business.

In some quarters there was even a decided lack of enthusiasm for retaining the JCRC as a unit. Within a few weeks of the collapse of South Vietnam, the Commander in Chief of Pacific Forces (CINCPAC) forwarded to the Joint Chiefs of Staff (JCS) in Washington DC a recommendation that the JCRC be deactivated. In its stead CINCPAC suggested that the Department of State assume the responsibilities for contact and negotiation with the Indochinese governments on the casualty resolution topic, that the Defense Intelligence Agency be responsible for updating and maintaining the casualty files and for the analysis of the information contained therein, and that the Army be tasked to maintain a capability to identify any recovered remains. JCS chose not to respond directly to these suggestions, and their reply of 27 June 1975 indicated only that the JCRC was to remain in its current location at Samae San, Thailand, for the time being.

Meanwhile, in response to a perceived need for a more long-range plan of action, the JCRC created a new division, the Negotiations Assistance Division, whose task was to prepare for eventual resumption of casualty resolution activity. A key factor in the JCRC preparation was the underlying assumption that nothing would, or could, take place until there was renewed contact between the US and Indochinese governments. JCRC's advocacy of such renewed contact was based on a number of factors. First, concern that the Vietnamese might take independent recovery actions without benefit of the required expertise and thus jeopardize the eventual identification of any recovered remains; second, the belief that the United States should take an active, rather than a reactive, stance regarding renewed talks to ensure that these discussions would avoid the adversarial environment which characterized the FPJMT meetings; and third, the fact that there were immediate casualty resolution tasks which needed to be addressed, such as the return of the remains of the two Marines killed at the time of the US evacuation from Saigon, and the return of the remains of those who had died while held captive in the south by the PRG.

The JCRC's advocacy efforts were not warmly welcomed. Nevertheless, largely in response to JCRC urging, the Office of the Secretary of Defense (OSD) convened a planning conference in August 1975 in Washington DC. This conference was attended by representatives from the offices of the Secretary of Defense, Secretary of State, JCS, CINCPAC, and the JCRC. Out of the conference deliberations came the decision that the JCRC (soon to shed its field teams, and reduced to slightly over 80 personnel) should prepare to assume the negotiation responsibilities previously held by the now-disestablished US delegation to the FPJMT; further, should negotiations begin (and it is debatable whether many of the attendees anticipated such a beginning) these negotiations would initially be conducted on the basis of Article 8(b) of the Paris Accords.

With a renewed lease on life and an expanded role, the JCRC began its planning efforts afresh in preparation for the time when the State Department could negotiate the reestablishment of discussions with the Indochinese governments on the issue of casualty resolution. Among the first tasks undertaken was the preparation of specialized dossiers on each missing individual carried in the JCRC files. These dossiers, which included a case summary written in narrative form, plus appropriate maps and photos, were intended to be passed to the Indochinese governments. The narratives contained all pertinent information about the circumstances of the loss incident available from the JCRC case records. It was hoped this would be later supplemented by additional information which the Indochinese governments might have gleaned from their own records. The total document package was intended to provide a "hot trail" or a starting point from which a Vietnamese or American investigator, for instance, could proceed to a particular village and interview witnesses and begin his own investigation into the particular loss incident. By mobilizing the JCRC staff (now augmented by those remaining JCRC members who had been evacuated from Saigon), and making a concerted effort, the majority of the case narratives were completed and translated by early 1976. Upon completion of the project, a total of 1,554 folders had been prepared, covering the loss circumstances of 2,613 individuals.

Assuredly, some within the Departments of Defense and State viewed with amazement the JCRC's frantic stirrings in anticipation of renewed casualty resolution effort. It was a time of skepticism, and many within the government doubted that the requisite steps leading to resumption of the effort would ever be taken. The JCRC activity, however, had an advocate in the person of Dr. Roger Shields, the Deputy Assistant Secretary of Defense for International Security and POW/MIA Affairs in Washington DC, whose duties included overseeing and providing guidance on casualty resolution matters. As a consequence, the JCRC found itself in frequent direct communication with this office, a situation which led to heightened strains between JCRC and its immediate headquarters, CINCPAC.[2]

Meanwhile, other factors were at work. Because of the changing political situation in Southeast Asia, the government of Thailand was moving to close former US-occupied bases, and negotiations were underway to implement the departure of the residual US force from Thailand. As units were withdrawn and bases were closed, the question again arose as to the fate of the JCRC and the Army's Central Identification Laboratory (CIL). CINCPAC suggested both should move back to the continental United States; JCRC made the recommendation to move to the Philippines; and the American embassy in Thailand recommended movement from Samae San to Bangkok. The Department of State made the call: retain both the JCRC and the CIL in Thailand for at least one more year with the preferred location at U-Tapao Air Base. The stated rationale for the decision was that the casualty resolution issue had caught the attention of

Congress, that a one-year congressional review was underway, and that Congress was taking a serious interest in the JCRC work.

THE ROLE OF CONGRESS

On 11 September 1975, the House of Representatives directed the formation of a Congressional Select Committee on Missing Persons in Southeast Asia. The House, both as an institution and as individual members, had previously maintained an interest in the topic of the missing in action. Beginning in the late 1960s, a number of relevant hearings had been conducted to investigate the topic and to keep House members apprised of the current state of affairs as attempts were being made to disengage from the Vietnam conflict. These hearings were ordinarily conducted by subcommittees of either the House Armed Services Committee or the House Foreign Affairs Committee. However, the newly established Select Committee cut across committee lines and was composed of 10 members of Congress complemented by a small investigative and administrative staff, with Congressman G. V. "Sonny" Montgomery (D-MS) designated as Committee Chairman. The Select Committee was initially given a life span of 12 months. It was tasked to "conduct a full and complete investigation and study of (1) the problem of US servicemen still identified as missing in action, as well as those known dead whose bodies have not been recovered, as a result of military operations in (Indochina) . . . and (2) the need for additional international inspection teams to determine whether there are servicemen still held as prisoners of war or civilians held captive or unwillingly detained . . . "[3] (The Select Committee charter was later paraphrased: "To study, investigate, and report on the problems of Americans still unaccounted for as a result of hostilities in Indochina."[4] The Committee final report did not

Members of the House Select Committee on Missing Persons met with Vietnamese officials in Hanoi in late 1975. Left to right: Congressman McCloskey (partially visible), Vice Foreign Minister Phan Hien, Congressman Montgomery (Committee chairman), Prime Minister Pham Van Dong, Congressman Gilman. Congressman Ottinger, not shown, was also a member of the party.

address the subject of the need for "additional international inspection teams.")

The committee immediately set to work, holding the first of many hearings on 23 September. In the following months, the committee and its small staff compiled an impressive record. Twenty-four open hearings and 17 private sessions were held with over 50 individuals called to testify. Committee and staff members also interviewed an additional 150 persons to gather data related to issues under study. Committee members met with a number of high-level officials, including both President Ford and Secretary of State Kissinger, to clarify specific areas. Views were solicited from family members of those still missing, from former prisoners of war, from administration officials, and from a wide range of individuals with particular interest and/or technical expertise on the question of persons still unaccounted for.

Committee staffers reviewed and examined in detail the case files of a large number of casualties in order to understand the circumstances surrounding the losses, as well as other factors bearing on their current legal status. The efforts by both the Departments of Defense and State were reviewed and analyzed. Visits were made and briefings received at the Joint Casualty Resolution Center and the Central Identification Laboratory in Thailand, as well as the pertinent offices of the Defense Intelligence Agency in Washington. Discussions were carried out with diplomatic officials from Bangkok, Beijing, Paris, and Geneva, among others.

Potentially the most significant of the Committee's efforts, however, were its discussions with government officials from Indochina. A visit to Hanoi and Vientiane by Congressman Montgomery and three other committee members in December 1975 served not so much to shed fresh light on the questions related to missing Americans, but rather to overcome bureaucratic inertia on the US side and to open the way for future and more meaningful discussions between United States and Indochinese officials. This visit was the first significant contact between US and Vietnamese officials following the communist takeover of South Vietnam and the evacuation of the Americans from Saigon earlier in the year.[5]

In many ways, the Hanoi visit also served as a vivid lesson regarding the manner in which the Vietnamese intended to handle the MIA issue, though no negotiations as such took place during the visit. When the Congressmen asked about the possibility of Americans being held anywhere in Vietnam, both Prime Minister Pham Van Dong and Deputy Foreign Minister Phan Hien stated emphatically that all American prisoners had been returned to United States custody in 1973. This answer, while arguably correct, considering the context in which the question was posed, was less than candid or adequate. At the time of their visit to Hanoi, committee members were unknowingly standing within 30 miles of American citizen Arlo Gay who was being held in a rural area prison west of Hanoi. United States Marine Robert Garwood was also residing in North Vietnam at that time, though probably not in the immediate vicinity of Hanoi.

Mr. Arlo Gay, who had worked in a private fishing venture in South Vietnam, was among those Americans arrested as the communist forces took over the country in May 1975. Suspicious of his background and activity, communist authorities transferred him to North Vietnam for further questioning and scrutiny. Mr. Gay was eventually released from incarceration in September 1976 and returned to the United States. PFC Robert Garwood, on the other hand, was well-known to Vietnamese authorities. He had been captured near Danang by the Viet Cong on 28 September 1965. After being held in various camps in South Vietnam, he was eventually moved to the north. Garwood, viewed by many as a collaborator with the Viet Cong, was not repatriated with other American prisoners in 1973, and subsequently became a part of the cadre that worked with the Vietnamese camp staff within the communist "re-education" camps established in northern Vietnam after 1975. In March 1979, at his own request, he was returned to US custody and was eventually court-martialed and discharged from military service by the US Marine Corps.

Congressman Montgomery's Select Committee visit also provided the Vietnamese officials an opportunity to press for economic assistance from the United States. The Vietnamese sought to link progress on the MIA issue (Article 8b of the Paris Accords) to US willingness to "heal the wounds of war" through contributions toward rebuilding the Vietnamese economy (as set forth in Article 21 of the Paris Accords). To the surprise of the visiting Congressmen, DRV officials also divulged the existence of a letter from President Nixon to Premier Pham Van Dong, and alleged that this letter represented a promise from the United States for 3.25 billion dollars' worth of reconstruction assistance.[6] Both Vietnamese officials urged the normalization of relations between the United States and the DRV, but Vice Minister Phan Hien specifically vetoed the idea of American involvement in the investigation of crash and grave sites, citing Vietnamese "public opinion" as a possible impediment to achieving progress.

DRV officials also used the congressional visit as an opportunity to hand over the remains of three US pilots who had been shot down while on missions over North Vietnam. The DRV had first made public their possession of these remains in a 22 April 1975 Hanoi radio broadcast and a subsequent letter to Senator Edward Kennedy (D-MA). In August, two days prior to a Security Council vote on UN membership for North and South Vietnam, the DRV notified the US government of their willingness to repatriate these three remains. When, on 11 August, the United States cast a vote which vetoed Vietnamese UN membership, the DRV immediately retracted their three-day-old offer to return the remains, citing the US lack of "goodwill."[7] Secretary of State Kissinger, in a speech to the Southern Governors Conference in Orlando on 16 September 1975, summed up the US reaction to this turn of events:

> I feel that they (the North Vietnamese) will use the missing in action for their political purposes, and we do not believe that American foreign policy should

be shaped by the holding of hostages—and even less
by the remains of Americans who died in action.[8]

Finally, on 6 December at their Embassy in Paris, the
DRV notified visiting Select Committee members of their
willingness to repatriate the three remains to their families through the Select Committee. Thus, in Hanoi on
21 December, nearly eight months to the day after their
announcement of possession of the remains, the DRV
released custody of these three remains to the visiting
Congressmen. The remains were duly escorted to the
Central Identification Lab in Thailand for positive identification and eventual return to their families for proper
burial.

The results of the Select Committee's investigative
efforts were documented in five sub-reports which detailed the conduct of the hearings and other committee
activity as it progressed. Upon expiration of the Select
Committee's charter (which had been extended from one
year to 15 months), a final report was submitted to the
House of Representatives on 13 December 1976. Among
the significant conclusions set forth in the report, perhaps
the most controversial, was that:

> the results of the investigations and information
> gathered during its 15-month tenure have led this
> committee to the belief that no Americans are still
> being held alive as prisoners in Indochina, or else-
> where, as a result of the war in Indochina.[9]

The committee also concluded that in many instances the
initial status classification (missing, killed, or captured)
was improper or questionable in light of the actual circumstances of loss. These findings, along with the Committee's belief that the current DOD procedures were
adequate and in conformance with the law, led to a committee recommendation that the Service Secretaries immediately resume case status reviews (previously
suspended by the DOD). Such a process would inevitably
result in recategorization of servicemen from a prisoner

or missing status to the status of KIA/BNR—killed in action, body not recovered.

The Select Committee reached another significant and controversial conclusion: "because of the nature and circumstances in which many Americans were lost in combat in Indochina, a total accounting by the Indochinese Governments is not possible and should not be expected."[10] The committee also concluded, however, that the Indochinese governments were capable of providing at least a partial accounting, based both upon information which they had or could obtain, and upon the recovery and repatriation of remains. In this regard, the committee report cited the expectation that "more than 150" remains could be returned. In order to implement this effort, the committee recommended that the State Department "promptly engage the governments of Indochina in direct discussions aimed at gaining the fullest possible accounting for missing Americans."[11]

As would be expected, the publication of the Committee's final report was met with varying, but spirited, reaction. Strangely, within the Select Committee itself there quickly appeared a number of "defectors." At the end of the final report, in its published form, were appended the "additional views" of committee member Congressman John Moakley (D-MA), as well as the "separate views" of members Benjamin Gilman (R-NY) and Tennyson Guyer (R-OH). Moakley, in his "additional views," contradicted the committee belief "that no Americans are still being held alive as prisoners in Indochina," stating that he believed the committee had gathered no evidence to either prove or disprove that all the missing were, in fact, dead. He also took issue with the committee's delving into the subject of status changes since, in his opinion, the committee had no jurisdiction in this area and therefore no right to make recommendations on this particular subject. Gilman and Guyer, in their "separate views," basically echoed these same concerns and reservations, but added their disagreement with the notion of the committee assigning a numerical value ("more than 150") to the amount of information or remains which the Indochinese governments might produce. They also made a strong plea for administration action, both to maintain the new momentum on the issue, and to make the necessary moves toward Vietnam to expedite eventual achievement of an accounting.[12]

Immediately following the printing of the report, Congressmen Richard Ottinger (D-NY) and Jim Lloyd (D-CA) made it known that they both associated themselves with the remarks of Congressman Moakley. Fully half of the ten Select Committee members had now made known their strong reservations or disagreements with the most important conclusions and recommendations put forth in the final committee report.

Family members were also extremely disturbed by the report; they perceived it to be a harbinger of a break in faith between the government and themselves. They found the recommendation to resume case status reviews, joined with the committee's "belief" that none of the missing were still alive, to be particularly onerous. First, it seemed that their own government was about to "write off" the casualties and put an end to all efforts to seek a final resolution of the cases. Second, many families were greatly offended by the report's emphasis on the topic of continued pay and allowances for the missing servicemen.[13] In their view, this impugned their motives and made the families appear as "money-grubbers" who were only interested in continuing the "missing" status of their loved ones for purposes of greed. In short, the families were unanimously disdainful of the report, and in their eyes Chairman Montgomery became the report personified. As a result, he was targeted for severe personal criticism by the relatives of the missing. Unfortunately, this feeling of ill will still persists today, and mention of Congressman Montgomery's name will draw derogatory remarks in any group of the next-of-kin.

The National League of Families of American Prisoners and Missing in Southeast Asia, acting on behalf of the family members, issued on 18 February 1977 their own analysis of the Select Committee's work.[14] This analysis was also highly critical of the committee's investigative effort and the final report. The committee was

accused of parroting administration positions and criti-
cized for a lack of independent or exhaustive investigation. Several committee members were accused of
tailoring the findings to fit their own preconceived notions
about the issue of servicemen still unaccounted for. In
light of the dissent expressed by half of the committee
members, the League also questioned the basic validity
of the committee's work. In addition, the League cited
Secretary Kissinger's lack of candor during discussions
with committee members regarding the letter sent earlier
by President Nixon to Vietnamese Prime Minister Pham
Van Dong as a basis for distrust of the motives and long-
range intentions of the US government on the casualty
resolution issue.[15] Finally, the League expressed its
amazement at what it termed "the wildly speculative be-
liefs and conclusions" contained in the final report. With
few exceptions the League found little to comfort the families or provide assurance of a future good faith effort on
the part of the government to resolve the fate of those still
unaccounted for.

In spite of the bad reviews received from family
members and their League, the Select Committee's work
was generally viewed by other elements of the US government in a more neutral or favorable light, depending
primarily on how the committee recommendations impacted on each organization. Both the Departments of
State and Defense escaped any serious criticism in the
committee report; hence, their reaction was generally
subdued. The State Department, in a message transmit-
ted on 16 December 1976, summarized the final report
conclusions and recommendations for the benefit of interested American embassies and missions. This summary
stressed, inter alia, that no Americans were still being
held alive as prisoners in Indochina. The summary also
took note of and described the views of dissenting committee members but, curiously, failed to report the specific disagreements of Congressmen Moakley and
Ottinger with the committee belief that there were no
live Americans still being held. In specific reaction to the
report, the State message went on to say that, "for our

part, we will continue our efforts to obtain an accounting for MIAs. We will also take into account the views of the Committee on negotiations (with the Indochinese governments).''[16]

The difference between institutional and personal views regarding the committee conclusions, and the eagerness with which some within government hoped the POW/MIA issue would subside or disappear was revealed in a letter written to Congressman Montgomery by a State Department official in January 1977. The writer stated, in part, that the Committee's final report was more than satisfactory:

> You and the Committee did a wonderful thing for our country when you made your findings so definitive. As you know, I agree with them totally. I hope now that the MIA mission is accomplished, the Congress will find another important project which will (bring us into contact) from time to time.''[17]

The Select Committee report was received favorably by the JCRC, though for other reasons. The JCRC headquarters, by the time the final committee report was published, had once again undergone the turmoil of relocation and further reduction of personnel. As the US-occupied bases in Thailand were shut down one by one, the unit was forced to move, first to U-Tapao Air Base, and then, in May 1976, to Barbers Point, Hawaii. Unit personnel strength was also reduced from approximately 80 down to 19. (Two of these personnel were permitted to remain behind in Thailand as the nucleus of a JCRC liaison office.) Included in the personnel reduction was the loss of the Negotiations Assistance Division and the downgrading of the unit commander's position from Brigadier General to Colonel, a move which CINCPAC had been unable to earlier implement.

The remaining JCRC personnel, all of whom had been eagerly awaiting any development which might spur new forward movement on the casualty resolution issue, took comfort from the Select Committee recommendations regarding resumption of contact between the US and Indochinese governments. Such contacts were viewed as a possible forerunner of on-site investigations which would hopefully lead to a final determination regarding the fate of those still missing. JCRC morale was further boosted by the recommendation that the State Department take advantage of JCRC expertise in their talks with the Indochinese governments. This was viewed as an opportunity to influence the State Department negotiators who did not fully appreciate what was needed physically or legally to assure resolution of a case, and so would not know exactly what to negotiate for.

Any executive branch action taken as a result of the Select Committee work, coinciding as it did with the conclusion of the Ford administration, would now be the responsibility of President Jimmy Carter. As a final parting act, indicative of the desire to put the Vietnam experience behind us, President Ford on 19 January 1977 ordered honorable discharges for approximately 700 deserters who had served in Vietnam and had either been wounded or decorated for valor. Two days later, and in keeping with his campaign promise, newly inaugurated President Carter ordered a "full, complete, and unconditional" blanket pardon for Vietnam draft evaders. And on 11 February 1977, three weeks after taking office, President Carter met with a delegation of six officers from the National League of Families, assuring them of his commitment to open talks between the United States and Vietnam in an effort to obtain an accounting for those servicemen and civilians still missing. In a move much favored by the League, the President also ordered the Defense Department to refrain from making unsolicited status changes until the United States had exhausted all avenues to obtain factual information regarding the fate of these individuals. In another move indicating a desire to quickly address unresolved issues between the Indochinese states and the United States, Carter shortly announced the pending dispatch of a Presidential Commission to Hanoi and Vientiane. The specific purpose of this commission was to seek further information on those still missing.

THE WOODCOCK COMMISSION

The Presidential Commission, publicly announced by the State Department on 25 February 1977, was given the following mandate:

> The Commission's primary purpose should be to obtain the best possible accounting for MIAs and the return of the remains of our dead. In addition, it should be authorized to obtain Vietnamese and Lao views on other issues and to report these views back to the President. But its mandate does not include authorization to engage in negotiations on the substance of these issues.[18]

President Carter selected Mr. Leonard Woodcock, President of the United Auto Workers, to head the five-member commission. Other commission members included former Senator Mike Mansfield, former Ambassador Charles Yost, Congressman Sonny Montgomery, and Mrs. Marian Wright Edelman, Director of the Children's Defense Fund (a Washington DC based child advocacy organization).

Even before its departure from Washington DC to Asia, the commission was the target of controversy. In an 18 February 1977 letter to National Security Advisor Zbigniew Brzezinski, the Executive Director of the National League of Families, Carol Bates, strongly appealed that Congressman Montgomery not be designated a commission member, basing her appeal on the League's view that Montgomery, in his earlier capacity as Chairman of the Congressional Select Committee, had misrepresented the conclusions and recommendations of that committee. In his 3 March reply to the League, Brzezinski noted the League's concern about Montgomery, but pointed to the need for a balanced group of commission members, a group "which must respond to a wide range of constituencies."

In their letter to Brzezinski, and later during a 7 March meeting with the commission members, League officials made a plea that a League member be included, at least as an observer, on the commission staff. This request was supported by many sympathetic congressmen, 45 of whom signed a letter to President Carter appealing that he include a POW/MIA family member in the group. The lack of administration response to this request, the inclusion of Congressman Montgomery as a commission member in spite of the families' objections, and the growing perception that the commission's real purpose was to set the stage for normalizing of relations with Vietnam at the expense of the MIA issue—all led to League suspicion that they were about to receive, once again, what they termed the "cosmetic treatment" by their own government.

On 13 March 1977 the five-member commission departed Washington DC for Southeast Asia, accompanied by eight staff members and a five-man press party. The group made a stop en route in Hawaii for briefings by DOD, the JCRC, and the Central Identification Laboratory (CIL); and to add three more members to the accompanying staff, all JCRC personnel. Following another overnight stop at Clark Air Base in the Philippines, the Commission landed at Gia Lam Airport near Hanoi on the afternoon of 16 March. The arriving commission was met by Vice Foreign Minister Phan Hien and a fleet of a dozen black state-owned cars. The group was immediately whisked off in formation across the Paul Doumer bridge—well known to American attack pilots—and into Hanoi to the government guest house to be greeted by Foreign Minister Nguyen Duy Trinh. As evidenced by the protocol, it was obvious that the now reunified Vietnam—the Socialist Republic of Vietnam (SRV)—was treating the commission visit as a serious matter.

During most of the discussions that took place in Hanoi on the ensuing three days, Deputy Foreign Minister Phan Hien was the primary SRV interlocutor. The commission and staff also met with Prime Minister Pham Van Dong, and a separate session was held between technical experts from both sides to specifically address the development and exchange of MIA information. In their presentations the SRV addressed three separate areas of concern between the United States and Vietnam: MIAs, normalization of diplomatic relations, and reconstruction aid. Phan Hien stressed that none of these three areas should be considered a precondition to the other two, but that all three were clearly interrelated.

Regarding MIAs, the SRV once again affirmed that "all American military personnel who had been taken prisoner during the Vietnam war and were still living, have been returned to the United States side" (proven to be erroneous when PFC Robert Garwood surfaced to be repatriated back to the United States two years later), and that "all Americans who remained in South Vietnam after 30 April 1975 and registered themselves with the Foreign Service of Vietnam, have been allowed to leave for their country."[19] In addition to affirming these previously stated positions, Phan Hien made the already-expected announcement that the SRV was prepared to repatriate the remains of 12 individuals which they had revealed some seven months earlier were in their possession. Later, during a somewhat ineffectual side-meeting of "experts," the SRV described in vague terms their unnamed specialized office to seek information on missing Americans and recover remains. General agreement was also reached on procedures to be used for exchanging data and information on Americans still missing. Though Vietnamese officials pledged to return to the United States any remains and all available information as soon as possible after they were discovered, the commission in its final report acknowledged that the SRV "almost certainly" had additional MIA information already available, but that it was not provided during the visit.

While an obligatory portion of the SRV presentation to the commission was devoted to the MIA topic, the subjects of US aid toward "healing the wounds of war" in Vietnam and normalizing of relations with the United States were obviously of greater interest to the hosts. As regards healing the wounds of war, Vietnamese officials referred to the "undeniable responsibility" of the United States for the destruction of Vietnam's economic base,

cultural establishments, natural resources, and the eco-
logical environment. Because of its singular responsibility
for this "atrocious war," said the SRV officials, the
United States had a legal and humanitarian obligation to
contribute to the postwar reconstruction of Vietnam.
Once again the Paris Accords were cited (Article 21, dealing with reconstruction), as well as the Nixon letter to
Pham Van Dong, as evidence of the US obligation to
provide the requested assistance. Magnanimously, SRV
officials agreed not only to welcome the US contribution
toward reconstruction, but also to "create favorable conditions for the United States to carry out this contribution."

Pham Van Dong, Foreign Minister Trinh, and Phan
Hien all spoke at some length on the topic of normalized
relations between the United States and Vietnam. In fact,
Phan Hien, in his remarks during the opening meeting
session, revealed how his government viewed the basic
purpose of the Presidential Commission visit when he
stated, "first of all I would like to say that we have this
opportunity to begin the process leading to the normalization of relations." Though the SRV officials noted that
obstacles still existed on the path to better relations, each
expressed the hope that the process of normalization
would move forward. Ultimately, during the final session
with the commission, Phan Hien proposed that normalization negotiations begin soon, either in Paris or Hanoi.

Despite the commission's full work schedule, there
were opportunities for lighter moments. The Vietnamese
hosts were exceedingly gracious and congenial, hosting a
grand banquet in honor of their visitors one evening, and
providing a first-rate musical show on a second night.
These events were duly recorded on film by the accompanying US media representatives, as were views of Congressman Montgomery and others during an early-
morning jogging session around the picturesque Hoan
Khiem Lake in the center of Hanoi. Unfortunately, when
these scenes were later played for US TV audiences, critics accused the commission of a lack of seriousness in

their mission, and of joining in a "love fest" with our former Vietnamese adversaries.

On the morning of 19 March 1977, just before the departure of the commission from Vietnam, a dignified repatriation ceremony was conducted on the hot tarmac at Gia Lam airport at which time the commission accepted custody of the remains of the 12 individuals believed by the SRV to be those of American servicemen.[20] The remains were loaded aboard the commission's C–141 aircraft, which then departed immediately for Vientiane, Laos, the next stop on the commission agenda.

Commission members, during their overnight stay in Vientiane, heard once again—this time from the Lao point of view—about the US obligation to assist in "healing the wounds of war" by helping reconstruct the country. Lao officials described in detail the difficulties encountered and their efforts to seek information and remains of American servicemen lost in Laos, but regretted they had no results to report to the commission. The Lao also denied the existence of any live captives still held as a consequence of the war.

Late on 20 March, the commission departed from Vientiane to begin the long journey back to Washington DC and to report the results of their visit to President Carter. In his oral report to the President, and as noted in the final written commission report, Chairman Woodcock expressed the view that a new and favorable climate had been created by the commission visit, and that the best hope for resolution of the MIA issue would be in the context of improved relations between the United States and the Indochinese states. Woodcock cited the creation of a "new spirit" as the most significant contribution toward the mission assigned to the commission by the President, mentioning the commission's belief that it had impressed upon Vietnam and Laos that the United States had a "realistic attitude" toward resolution of the MIA issue, and that it was the US intent to remove this issue as a barrier to normalization of relations. The commission expressed the view that a non-confrontational approach toward Vietnam and Laos would be more likely to elicit further cooperation on the MIA issue.

In addition to these general views, the commission report specifically concluded that, based upon the talks with Indochinese officials and on other information made available, ''there is no evidence to indicate that any American POWs from the Indochina conflict remain alive.'' The commission agreed with the Vietnamese that those Americans who had stayed in Vietnam after 30 April 1975 had now departed and found no evidence to support the occasional rumors of deserters still living in Indochina. The commission did concede, however, that the Vietnamese probably had other information on missing Americans which it did not reveal, but took seriously the Vietnamese assurance that they would search for further information and remains and would provide it promptly to the United States. The commission report also noted the ''new procedure'' which was established for the continuing exchange of MIA information between Vietnam and the United States. (Establishing this ''new procedure,'' in fact, amounted to no more than the exchange of mailing addresses between two points of contact in the US Department of State and the SRV Ministry of Foreign Affairs.)

Furthermore, the commission made a strong recommendation that the normalization process be vigorously pursued by a resumption of talks in Paris between US and Vietnamese representatives. The commission also recommended continued technical exchanges on accounting for MIAs, suggesting that US personnel deliver pertinent information to Hanoi and that Vietnamese representatives visit the US identification laboratory facilities in Hawaii. The US government was urged to promptly consider providing material assistance to aid Vietnamese search and recovery activity, and to encourage private American groups to increase humanitarian aid programs for Indochina in such areas as food, medical supplies, and prosthetic equipment.[21]

As with the work of the Congressional Select Committee which preceded it, the work of President Carter's

Commission met with immediate criticism. A White House news conference was held following Chairman Woodcock's report to the President. Press interest had been heightened by the President's earlier announcement of imminent resumption of negotiations in Paris between the United States and Vietnam for the purpose of establishing normalized relations with Hanoi. At the news conference, President Carter was questioned by reporters regarding his statements indicating complete satisfaction with the results of the commission's trip. In response to a reporter's suggestion that he had changed his position regarding the necessity for the Vietnamese to account for MIAs before normalization would be considered, the President expressed his belief that by returning the remains of American servicemen to the visiting commission, and by their agreement to investigate cases and exchange technical information relating to the losses, the Vietnamese had acted in a positive manner which would justify the opening of normalization talks. Referring to the Vietnamese, the President stated:

> "I think this is about all they can do. I don't have any way to prove that they have accounted for all of those about whom they have information. But I think, so far as I can discern, they have acted in good faith."[22]

Later, Chairman Woodcock was questioned closely by a phalanx of doubting congressmen when he reported the results of the commission efforts to the House International Relations Subcommittee on Asia and Pacific Affairs on 31 March 1977. The congressmen's questions and comments clearly implied both their distrust of Vietnamese intentions and motives, and their belief that the commission members had been "taken in" by their Vietnamese hosts. Congressman Benjamin Gilman (R-NY) took the commission to task, saying he did not share the sense of accomplishment or forward movement portrayed in the commission's written report. Congressman Herb Burke (R-FL), expressing suspicion of Vietnamese motives, thought that rather than acting in a purely humane manner, the Vietnamese government was presenting the United States with a "blackjack proposition" wherein Vietnamese cooperation on the MIA issue would be exchanged for US acquiescence on SRV membership in the United Nations. Congressman Frank Gooding (R-ID) was critical that no family members had been included on the commission. Congressman Robert Lagomarsino (R-CA) considered that the commission should have brought up the subject of Vietnamese human rights violations in the course of the discussions in Hanoi. Finally, several congressmen expressed their revulsion at associating the accounting of missing American servicemen with the provision of aid to Vietnam, and the lifting of the trade embargo.

As an aside, in a gesture·which many family members would have expected, at this same hearing commission member Congressman Sonny Montgomery once again advocated that the President should proceed with case reviews and should declare all MIAs as killed in action. With what some would view as almost callous indifference, Montgomery argued that this would relieve the servicemen's families of the anguish associated with their uncertain status.

Columnist John P. Roche, in an article published in the *Washington Star* on 1 April 1977, took Woodcock to task for his apparent naiveté, likening the commission's Hanoi trip to "a visitation by the Salvation Army to the Mafia." The League of Families, in a "position paper" commenting on the commission efforts, drew similar parallels, but in less colorful language and with less cynicism.[23] The League paper expressed disappointment over the commission's failure to return with substantive information about those still unaccounted for. While the League of Families agreed that the repatriation of remains brought about by the commission's visit was a step forward, they also viewed this activity as far less than what the Vietnamese were capable of doing had they exhibited a truly cooperative attitude. The League was encouraged by the announcement that the United States intended to enter into bilateral talks with the Vietnamese

on the MIA issue, but expressed skepticism regarding
Vietnam's willingness to work within the bounds of the
"technical mechanism" established by the commission.

Even among the participating staff members of the
commission there was a feeling that the results fell far
short of what was being indicated by the optimistic statements of Chairman Woodcock, echoed by the President.
Dr. Roger Shields, the Deputy Assistant Secretary of Defense for International Security Affairs, who had represented the Secretary of Defense on the commission staff,
filed a critical report of the commission's efforts. He
pointed out that the turnover of remains to the commission represented "the minimal response which we could
have expected from the Vietnamese."[24] He argued that
in spite of Vietnamese assurances to the commission that
they had no further remains or knowledge about any US
missing persons, abundant and unambiguous information possessed by the United States, much of it already
made public, proved the contrary. From this, Dr. Shields
concluded that the Victnamese were continuing to link
progress on accounting for US casualties to resolution of
economic and political issues. Dr. Shields also made clear
that he viewed the upcoming discussions in Paris as a test
of Vietnamese good faith. Regarding resumption of case
reviews, he recommended that any status changes (from
MIA to KIA, for example) be held in abeyance pending
the outcome of the Paris talks, with a review of this recommendation once Vietnamese intentions become more
clear. A State Department official, also a staff member
on the commission, wrote of his doubts about the commission results in a 6 April 1977 letter to another officer:
"We have been appearing repeatedly on the Hill with
Woodcock et al. Mostly sweetness and light . . . which
worries me. What will they say six months from now
when nothing has happened?"

In retrospect, it is difficult to assess the impact of
the Woodcock Commission. On the plus side, the effort
seemed, once again, to momentarily stir the Vietnamese
to renewed activity on the MIA issue. The remains repatriation on the occasion of the commission's visit to Hanoi

was followed six months later by another repatriation, when the remains of 22 Americans who had died in Vietnam were returned. (This repatriation followed by ten days the admission of Vietnam into the United Nations on 20 September 1977. Rather than veto Vietnam's membership in the UN as in the past, the United States abstained during the vote.)

Unfortunately, the so-called mechanism which was established by the Woodcock Commission to enhance the technical exchange of casualty resolution information, based as it was on communications via the State Department in Washington DC, never proved to be a viable conduit for exchange of data at the technical level. File information was passed to the SRV, along with requests for verification or supplemental information, but there were no substantive responses received.

The Woodcock Commission, because it laid heavy emphasis on avoidance of controversy or confrontation and had refrained from any aggressive push for MIA answers, probably deluded SRV officials into believing that the United States was prepared to normalize relations at any cost. This belief by SRV officialdom, in the long run, may have delayed more meaningful cooperation on resolving the MIA issue. In addition, some might argue that by not taking a ''hard-line'' approach in its discussions with the SRV, the commission may also have overly emboldened the Vietnamese who then pursued a less cautious approach in dealings with their Asian neighbors. Regardless of what may or may not have been the true legacy of the Woodcock Commission, the families of those still missing perceived the commission as evidence of a Carter policy of ''normalization first, casualty resolution later,'' a policy which the families felt would forfeit US leverage on the MIA issue. Thus, in the eyes of these families, the Carter administration suffered an early blow to its reputation and its credibility in dealing with the issue of the MIAs—a blow from which it never fully recovered.

THE MOVE TOWARD US-VIETNAM NORMALIZATION

Immediately on the heels of the Woodcock Commission visit, direct talks began between US and Vietnamese officials. The first round of discussions, intended to lead ultimately to normalization of diplomatic relations, took place in Paris on 3 and 4 May 1977. While the US side was only prepared to normalize relations without preconditions, the Vietnamese side, led by Mr. Phan Hien, once again brought up the topic of reconstruction assistance and cited the 1973 Nixon letter as a commitment for aid. SRV officials apparently underestimated US officials' repugnance toward the idea of "reparations," and American reaction to SRV use of this emotionally charged word during the discussions. Even those Americans who might have been favorably disposed toward better relations with Vietnam found it politically unpalatable to move forward as long as Vietnamese demands were couched in such terms. This Vietnamese insistence on "reparations" as a part of the normalization process, reiterated during a second round of talks begun on 2 June, effectively precluded any forward movement toward a mutual agreement. Only during the third round of talks, begun on 19 December 1977, did Vietnamese officials finally back away from their demand for aid as a precondition to normalization; however, Phan Hien again urgently sought an informal commitment from US negotiator Richard Holbrooke that aid would follow as a consequence of normalization. Holbrooke's inability to provide such a commitment led to adjournment of the talks.

Though President Carter had hoped to put the Vietnam War era behind, as clearly evidenced by his early unconditional pardon of the draft dodgers and by his implied assent to SRV United Nations membership, subsequent events led to a further chilling of the climate between the United States and Vietnam. In February 1978, just before the start of a planned fourth round of normalization talks, an American official of the US Information Agency and an American-Vietnamese associate were arrested by the FBI on charges of spying for the SRV. Implicated in the case was the Vietnamese UN Ambassador in New York, Dinh Ba Thi, who was quickly declared persona non grata and expelled from the United States.[25] As a consequence of the ensuing ill feelings, the fourth series of negotiations were indefinitely postponed.

By the summer of 1978, however, emotions had calmed and the SRV once again moved to establish a relationship with the United States. In mid-July, in response to an earlier US invitation, the SRV dispatched a team of officials for a four-day trip to the facilities of the JCRC and Central Identification Laboratory (CIL) in Hawaii. The group was briefed on US methods of crash site and gravesite excavation, was shown the extent of US casualty files, and participated in discussions on analysis techniques. They also witnessed the anthropological capabilities and methods used in the laboratory to identify repatriated remains.

This visit to Hawaii by the SRV delegation was followed shortly by a Vietnamese announcement of the discovery and pending repatriation of the remains of another 11 American servicemembers. This time, Vietnamese officials used the occasion of another congressional delegation's visit to Hanoi to return the remains to US custody.[26] This delegation, led by Congressman Sonny Montgomery, received the remains on 26 August at Gia Lam airport, just across the river east of Hanoi.

Meanwhile, plans were being quietly made to meet once again with Vietnamese negotiators, this time in the UN offices in New York. On 22 September, and again on 27 September, Mr. Holbrooke met with Deputy Foreign Minister Nguyen Co Thach. During the latter session Thach finally clearly agreed that normalization could proceed without a prior commitment on the part of the United States for reconstruction assistance and aid. Of this sudden reversal on the part of Vietnamese officials following years of protracted discussions, Holbrooke is alleged to have commented, ''Bang! In one go Thach laid it all out. Then he wanted the agreement, which could not be signed for two years, to be settled in ten minutes.''[27]

In spite of the concession by the SRV on the contentious point of a US promise of assistance, other events were to overtake the move toward normalization. In late June 1978, at Russia's strong urging, Vietnam had joined the Council for Mutual Economic Assistance (COMECON), the Soviet dominated Socialist economic group. This, plus indications of significantly heightened tensions between Vietnam and neighboring Cambodia, gave reason for suspicion as to Vietnam's future intentions. Moreover, ethnic Chinese were by this time fleeing persecution in Vietnam by the boatload, prompting public and official US indignation toward Vietnam and drawing unfavorable congressional attention. Perhaps most significant of all, however, was the fact that negotiations were proceeding secretly but rapidly toward establishment of full diplomatic relations between the United States and China. President Carter had become convinced that normalization with China was of more lasting significance to US interests, and that normalization could not be simultaneously concluded with China and Vietnam. Thus, in October 1978, Carter decided to delay any normalization with Vietnam until after the establishment of full relations with China.

The events which followed are a matter of record. On 3 November 1978 Vietnam and the Soviet Union tightened their embrace by concluding a Treaty of Friendship and Cooperation. On Christmas Day the sporadic fighting between Vietnamese and Khmer Rouge forces on the Vietnam-Cambodia border areas finally erupted into all-out conflict between these communist neighbors as the Vietnamese launched a full-scale invasion into Cambodia. The Vietnamese forces swept westward across Cambodia, hardly hesitating at the capital of Phnom Penh and pushing ahead of them the retreating Khmer Rouge forces of Pol Pot. Within less than two months China, the backer of the Khmer Rouge, retaliated by attacking Vietnam at numerous points along the Vietnamese northern frontier. The United States, neither wanting to give the impression of condoning Vietnam's invasion of Cambodia, nor wanting to jeopardize the impending normalization with China, put an indefinite hold on any further moves toward normalization of relations with Hanoi.

For the Carter administration, the key to resolution of the issue of those missing in action was the normalization of relations with Hanoi. Administration officials believed that only with the normalization process would come the Vietnamese cooperation needed to learn the fate of those still unaccounted for. While this view was disputed by many of the family members speaking through the League of Families, it was the view that prevailed. President Carter had begun his administration with a plan to speedily normalize relations, and seemingly expected that the issue of missing American servicemen would just as speedily be resolved and would fade from view as an issue to be dealt with. Protracted Vietnamese insistence on "reparations", combined with the Carter decision to push forward first on the normalization with China, however, delayed administration efforts to achieve normalized relations until too late. A multitude of events had coincided to halt the momentum toward achievement of a reconciliation with Hanoi. This failure to achieve normalization marked the beginning of a lengthy period of further diminished progress toward a full accounting for the fate of those still missing.

NOTES

1. At the time of the fall of South Vietnam, approximately 100 remains had been recovered and identified as those of Americans. This number included the 23 remains of those who had died while in captivity in North Vietnam, repatriated from Hanoi in March 1974.

2. In January 1976, CINCPAC felt obliged to address the topic of JCRC's direct contacts with Washington DC and, in a message to the Joint Chiefs of Staff, asked that in the future all communications to JCRC from Washington DC be directed

through CINCPAC. In a reply two days later, JCS advised that they had discussed the matter with OSD/ISA, and future communication would be in accordance with the wishes of CINCPAC. While this appeared to be a relatively minor matter, it was symptomatic of a greater problem underlying the entire relationship between the JCRC and its headquarters. This relationship, unfortunately, was not to be smoothed over merely by a single message to the JCS.

3. US House of Representatives, Hearings Before the Select Committee on Missing Persons in Southeast Asia, Part 1 (94th Congress, 1st Session), p. ii.

4. US House of Representatives, Select Committee on Missing Persons in Southeast Asia, Final Report, dated 13 December 1976 (94th Congress, 2d Session, House Report no. 94-1764), p. 5.

5. In addition to Select Committee Chairman Congressman Sonny Montgomery (D-MS), others who participated in this trip to Hanoi included Congressmen Richard Ottinger (D-NY), Benjamin Gilman (R-NY), and Paul McCloskey (R-CA); and several staff personnel.

6. The letter from President Nixon to Prime Minister Pham Van Dong became a subject of considerable controversy. This letter, dated 1 February 1973, was alleged by the DRV to promise that (a) the US government would contribute to postwar reconstruction in North Vietnam without any political conditions, (b) US preliminary studies indicated that the appropriate programs would fall in the range of 3.25 billion dollars of grant aid over a period of 5 years, and (c) other forms of aid would be agreed upon between the two parties. While DRV officials portrayed this letter as a firm and unconditional US commitment, both President Nixon and Secretary Kissinger took a different view. They contended that the letter did not contain any pledges or promises of aid, but rather represented US willingness to participate in postwar reconstruction as specified in Article 21 of the Paris Accords, and advised the DRV of the preliminary financial estimates of the composition of the reconstruction program. They also contended that there was a definite US-DRV understanding that congressional authorization and appropriation would be a prerequisite to any implementation of such a reconstruction program.

Executive branch refusal to provide a copy of the letter to the Select Committee for its examination led to committee suspicion that there was some form of "secret agreement" or quid pro quo which might impact on Vietnamese cooperation on the MIA issue. This suspicion was eventually shared by the families of the missing, and reinforced their distrust of administration efforts to resolve the MIA issue.

With the agreement of the NSC, the complete text of the letter was finally released by the State Department on 19 May 1977. Examination of the letter indicates that it was indeed what it was represented to be by Nixon and Kissinger—not the unqualified "promise" which Vietnamese officials led visiting congressmen to believe. In fairness to the Vietnamese, however, it is not difficult to imagine that the letter, written as it was in rather stilted "bureaucratese", could be either wrongly or wishfully interpreted as a written commitment for a specific amount of postwar reconstruction assistance. Considering the probable reason that the letter was written in the first place, it should have come as no great surprise to US officials that the Vietnamese interpreted it as a promise.

7. According to Secretary of State Kissinger, the US veto of UN membership for the DRV and the PRG was not directed as a hostile act toward Vietnam. The action, he said, was taken to uphold the right of UN membership for worthy non-communist states, a right which had been denied to South Korea several days earlier when on 6 August 1975 their application for UN membership had been refused Security Council consideration.

8. Department of State Bulletin, vol. 73, no. 1893, 6 October 1975, p. 520.

9. US House of Representatives, Select Committee on Missing Persons in Southeast Asia, Final Report, dated 13 December 1976 (94th Congress, 2d Session, House Report no. 94-1764), p. vii. In addition to the quoted conclusions, the committee arrived at a number of other lesser conclusions, most of which have been proved valid during the intervening 16 years since the committee report was issued.

10. Ibid., p. vii.

11. Ibid., p. vii.

12. Ibid. For Congressman Moakley's views, see pp. 255-256. For the views of Congressmen Gilman and Guyer, see pp. 257-259.

13. Individuals carried in the status of "missing" are deemed, in a legal sense, to be still on active duty. Thus they, or their designated next-of-kin, are entitled to receive their full pay and allowances. Once this status is changed from "missing" to a presumptive finding of death, the pay and allowances cease and the legally stipulated survivor benefits begin, normally at a significantly reduced monetary value.

14. The National League of Families of American Prisoners and Missing in Southeast Asia, *Analysis of the Final Report of the House Select Committee on Missing Persons in Southeast Asia*, 18 February 1977.

15. For elaboration on the Nixon letter to Prime Minister Pham Van Dong, refer to note 6 above.

16. State Department message 305388, DTG 162258Z Dec 76.

17. The author of the 18 January 1977 letter to Congressman Montgomery will remain unnamed, lest he share with the congressman the same slings and arrows delivered by the family members and by the National League of Families. .

18. The specific mandate of the Presidential Commission was quoted in a 16 March 1977 letter from National Security Advisor Brzezinski to the Executive Director of the National League of Families.

19. Quoted from an 18 March 1977 SRV Aide-Memoire provided to the commission upon their departure from Vietnam. Meeting notes indicate that Phan Hien, under questioning, added another caveat when he stated that "all those who registered themselves *and who have asked to leave* have been allowed to leave."

20. Of the 12 remains repatriated, 11 were positively identified as those of American servicemen. In the twelfth case, the remains were determined to be those of a Vietnamese individual, and arrangements were made to return these remains back to Hanoi during another repatriation visit six months later.

21. Report of the Presidential Commission's Trip to Vietnam and Laos, March 16-20, 1977.

22. President Carter's comments are quoted from a UPI account of his news conference held at the White House on 24 March 1977.

23. *Position Paper of the National League of Families of American Prisoners and Missing in Southeast Asia*, April 1977.

24. Undated memo for the Secretary of Defense, Reference number I-5135/77, Subject: Presidential Commission on the Missing in Action, signed by Roger E. Shields.

25. For an interesting account of the spying incident which led to the expulsion of the SRV Ambassador to the UN, see Nayan Chanda's book, *Brother Enemy* (San Diego: Harcourt Brace Jovanovich, Publishers, 1986), pp. 154-156 and pp. 267-269.

26. Congressman Montgomery's delegation spent several days visiting both Hanoi and Vientiane to discuss the MIA issue. On 26 August 1978, the delegation flew to both cities in an Air Force C–141 and picked up the 11 remains in Hanoi, plus another four remains in Vientiane.

27. Nayan Chanda, *Brother Enemy,* p. 266.

3

HEIGHTENED ACTIVITY

REFUGEES STREAM FROM INDOCHINA

With the helicopter evacuation from the roofs of Saigon in the early morning hours of 30 April 1975 came the end of the official American presence in Vietnam. The unofficial presence included an assortment of journalists, humanitarian workers, and a few others who remained in Vietnam of their own free will, together with a number of other American citizens who wanted to leave but, for various reasons, were unfortunate enough to miss the final evacuation. All these people, with several notable exceptions, were gradually rounded up by the new communist regime and expelled from Vietnam, with the bulk of them leaving from Saigon in the summer of 1976.

The departure of the official American community from Vietnam had a decided impact on the efforts being made to resolve the fate of those servicemen still not accounted for. Most immediately affected were on-going activities which were directed toward searching the South Vietnamese countryside for aircraft crashsites and possible gravesites. Such activity, however, had already been

69

considerably curtailed as a result of the heightened insecurity throughout the countryside, particularly as hostilities had built toward the final communist push for
takeover of the south. An even more significant and lasting result of the American departure was the loss of access
to the Vietnamese populace, the only real source of potentially useful information needed to determine the fate of
the missing, barring cooperation of the Indochinese governments.

The residual Americans were not the only ones who
were apprehensive as the North Vietnamese army made
its final thrust toward Saigon. Fearing stern reprisals at
the very least, thousands of Vietnamese citizens were desperate to flee and escape life under the communist yoke.
While many were evacuated by the Americans in the days
just before the final takeover and some escaped aboard
commandeered aircraft, a larger number eventually took
to any available boat and fled by sea to the neighboring
southeast Asian countries.

This stream of refugees, initially a trickle of people,
gradually increased in reaction to the new government's
repressive economic and political measures. A blanket of
despair began to settle over the country. When, in March
1978, the Vietnamese government suddenly imposed severe sanctions against ethnic Chinese throughout the
country, and particularly in Chinese enclaves such as the
Cho Lon section of Saigon, the trickle of refugees quickly
turned into a flood. To cope with this influx of refugees,
temporary camps sprang up almost overnight in the
neighboring countries of Thailand, Malaysia, Indonesia,
Singapore, and the Philippines, as well as the colonies
of Hong Kong and Macau. The effort to relocate these
refugees to new homes on a permanent basis began in
earnest, prompting the creation of what was soon to become a new and bustling industry in Southeast Asia: that
of refugee processing and resettlement.

To those working on the issue of missing Americans,
these refugees, newly departed from their former homeland, constituted a potentially useful source of information about what was transpiring back in their native

country. Military personnel in the JCRC Liaison Office in Bangkok were eager to begin searching among the refugees for scraps of information which might bear on the fate of missing Americans. It soon became obvious, however, that using the refugees as information sources would not be easy, and US government efforts to exploit this opportunity got off to a sputtering start as the ever-increasing stream of refugees began to take on a political dimension.

The Indochinese were not particularly welcome in any of the neighboring countries, and were viewed as a disrupting influence in the existing society. In the case of Thailand, for instance, there was no love lost between the Thais and the Vietnamese. Thailand was not eager to have these refugees on its soil, and was anxious that they either return to their homeland, or be immediately taken out of Thailand by the international community and settled elsewhere. Moreover, the host countries generally resented the added financial burden of maintaining the camps, in spite of the assistance which was being provided under the auspices of the United Nations High Commissioner for Refugees (UNHCR). With few exceptions the host countries made sure that conditions within the camps were exceedingly spartan to discourage other potential refugees from following. These conditions, as well as other factors, all had a bearing on whether or not access could be gained to interview refugees of interest. Because the camps were not on US territory, American personnel who desired to interview the refugees were dependent on the goodwill of the host country to gain entry to the refugee camps, and the host country was not always eager to have Americans wandering in the camps to view the harsh and sometimes even severe conditions imposed on the camp residents.

Given the limited staff of the JCRC and other organizations charged with gathering and analyzing MIA information, it was clearly impossible to conduct a detailed interview of each and every refugee throughout Asia regarding his knowledge of missing Americans. Consequently, a plan was devised and implemented to pinpoint those who had specific information of interest, then to interview them in detail to acquire whatever information they possessed. This plan began with an effort to heighten all refugees' awareness of the US government's desire for MIA-related information. Multi-language posters, in Vietnamese, Lao, Khmer, Hmong, Chinese, Thai, and English, were placed in prominent locations around the refugee camps. The word was also passed by making periodic loudspeaker broadcasts to the camp populace, and through word of mouth using the refugee leadership within each camp. The message to the refugee community was simple: following a brief explanation of the US effort to locate Americans yet unaccounted for as a result of the war in Indochina, the refugee was urged that

> if you have any information about (a) Americans living freely or in captivity in your home country, (b) burial sites which may contain the remains of Americans, or (c) aircraft crashsites which may contain the remains of Americans, please notify. . .

The designated point of contact was ordinarily the US refugee resettlement officials and workers who were present in the camps on a daily basis. In this way, officials quickly identified a number of leads and interviewed them in detail during regular periodic visits to all the refugee camps.

Expanding the refugee interview program throughout the Asian area was not without its problems. In addition to coordination problems with gaining host government approval for camp access, other significant problems arose, many of our own making. One of the first debates came about over the question of active solicitation of POW/MIA information. Most US officials found no fault with making refugees aware of the US desire for any information which might assist in resolving the uncertainty regarding those Americans still missing, and of affording these refugees the opportunity to voluntarily report this information to an American representative. A few officials, however, expressed grave concern over the concept of actively going among the refugees, interviewing them individually, and specifically asking whether or not they had such information of interest. These officials feared that refugees would seize upon the idea that the key to attaining resettlement in the United States would be to claim knowledge of missing Americans. This situation, they suggested, would lead to a rash of fabricated stories. In several countries, other problems delayed implementation of an aggressive refugee interview program. In one instance, for example, the responsible refugee officer was initially unwilling to agree to camp interviews, suggesting rather that the Department of Defense conduct detailed interviews only after the refugees had been resettled to the United States. Again, his concern seemed to center on the possibility of creating an incentive to generate false information. "I also am not keen on DOD types going into (the camps) to interview refugees. I propose that we let DOD have a crack at them upon arrival in CONUS," he wrote.[1]

Another problem initially encountered in two countries involved the young US-contracted refugee workers (usually referred to as members of the JVA—Joint Voluntary Agencies), many of whom were a part of the anti-war generation and were openly antagonistic toward US government efforts to seek information about missing servicemen. Some felt that they, along with the whole refugee resettlement program, were being politicized by the MIA issue, and strongly vocalized their unwillingness to address any questions to the refugees. Only very slowly was this initial uncooperativeness overcome as a result of a considerable "public relations" effort by JCRC interviewers. To the JVA workers' credit, once they became convinced of the worth of the effort, they became some of the most aggressive and effective supporters of the information gathering program.

Despite such problems, active solicitation was begun, with the full understanding that there indeed would be a certain number of false leads. The JCRC interviewers and others working to gather information simply adopted the attitude that they would accept the story of the refugee, although not without the benefit of as detailed an interview as possible. The interview results would be reported, and would then become a matter for trained analysts to verify or disprove. Essentially, this was an acknowledgement that we must accept some chaff in order to obtain the wheat—the burden of sorting out which was which fell to the analysts.

MIA REPORTS FLOW IN

From its beginning in Thailand, the refugee interview program expanded throughout the various camp areas in Southeast Asia, trying to keep pace with the ever-increasing numbers of refugees fleeing from Vietnam, Laos, and Cambodia. As the Vietnamese government increased the pressure and intimidation against ethnic Chinese residing in Vietnam in mid-1978, and as uncertainty increased as a result of the Vietnamese invasion of Cambodia, the flight of people to neighboring countries markedly increased. At its peak, the outflow reached the phenomenal number of approximately 64,000 Vietnamese who fled their homeland during the month of May 1979—nearly all by boat.[2]

Personnel of the small JCRC Liaison Office in Bangkok had become involved in the detailed interviewing of refugees almost from the time of the establishment of this office in 1976. At that time the refugees were predominantly Lao and Hmong who had crossed the Mekong River into Thailand from Laos, along with a relatively small number of Vietnamese who had trickled out of Vietnam and reached the Thai coast by boat. As the refugee flow increased, however, particularly with the flood of "boat people" from Vietnam in 1979, the tempo of interview activity increased. Though screening and interviewing of refugees by others began earlier, the JCRC did not become heavily involved in this task in Malaysia, Singapore, and Indonesia until 1979. Thereafter, JCRC interview activity expanded to the camps of Hong Kong, Macau, and the Philippines, as well as occasionally to Japan and China.

As the refugee camp population grew, and as more personnel became involved, the number of information reports forwarded for analysis and possible correlation to missing Americans steadily increased. From approximately 400 reports in 1979, the JCRC wrote nearly 1,000 information reports in 1985 and in the years that have followed. It must also be pointed out that, in addition to the JCRC, others were similarly involved in collecting relevant information about Americans still unaccounted for. The entire official American community was activated to seek out and report any and all information which might pertain to those still missing. In Asia, information was gathered and reported not only by the JCRC, but also by elements of the Defense Intelligence Agency (DIA), the Central Intelligence Agency (CIA), the State Department, and the Justice Department.

In those cases where it was not possible to conduct a detailed interview before the refugee's departure for resettlement, appropriate arrangements were made to conduct the interview at a later date. This was not an uncommon event in those instances where the refugee was unexpectedly resettled rapidly, or where he did not make known his knowledge about missing Americans until after he had already moved to his new homeland. In such cases, the detailed interviews were ordinarily conducted by employees of DIA, or by members of the various investigation offices of the military services. In the event refugees had resettled to countries other than the United States, interviews were commonly conducted by personnel from the Defense Attaché Office of the corresponding American Embassy. Consequently, over the years former Indochinese residents have been interviewed in such diverse places as Paris, Bahrain, Stockholm, Osaka, and Perth.

While refugees have constituted the primary and perhaps most useful source of new information about the fate of missing Americans, they are by no means the sole source of such information. Foreign diplomats posted to the countries of Vietnam, Laos, and Cambodia have often been willing to volunteer information which they have gleaned, either from personal observation, or from conversations with host country officials or civilians. One such instance occurred when a western ambassador to Hanoi while passing through Bangkok, reported to the JCRC Liaison Officer that he had spotted a black man attired in native dress and riding a bicycle in the town of Gia Lam directly across the river from Hanoi. The ambassador speculated that the man may have been an American, perhaps a former serviceman, who had opted to remain in Vietnam. (For lack of any additional clarifying details or evidence, no definitive conclusion was ever drawn regarding this report.) Similar cooperation in sharing information has also been obtained from businessmen, tourists, newspersons, and other travelers to these countries, all of whom have been sympathetic toward efforts to resolve the MIA issue.

As one would expect, the collected reports have varied widely in specificity, content, and degree of detail. The information has ranged from firsthand knowledge of burial locations or sightings of Americans, to the vaguest of rumors of aircraft crashsites or grave sites. Some reports have included amazing amounts of detail, while others are so nebulous as to be nearly useless. Nevertheless, the analysts of both the JCRC and the DIA have undertaken the task of attempting correlation of the reports, trying to piece together the over 2,000 picture puzzles which represent the complete story of the fate of missing Americans. In some instances, most of the puzzle pieces are in place and a clear picture has already emerged. In many other instances, though, only a few pieces are in place and much more needs to be done before we can gain an understanding of what happened to a particular individual.

In any event, nothing is discarded by the analysts. Information which does not immediately fit into the picture may at some later date become explainable as more

This bas-relief on a factory wall in Hanoi reports the shootdown of an American aircraft. JCRC and DIA analysts evaluated clues such as this in their efforts to determine the fate of missing Americans.

and more information is gathered and analyzed. For example, there was a flurry of reports from diplomats posted in Hanoi in mid-1976 regarding vague rumors of the escape from prison of an alleged bearded American pilot POW. These reports made little sense until later when more was learned of the experiences of American citizen Arlo Gay (mentioned earlier) who had been held captive near Hanoi. Gay had indeed escaped into the North Vietnamese foothills for nearly four weeks, and was the subject of an intense manhunt before being again taken into custody. Gay was eventually released in September 1976.

Unquestionably the quality of the information gathered has varied widely. Firsthand accounts have generally been more detailed than hearsay information, particularly as the hearsay is passed through more and more ''tellers''. Some informants have proven to possess excellent memories, while others can recollect very few details. The interviewers have been faced with the task of eliciting as much information as possible, in as much detail as possible, without leading the informant or suggesting answers to questions posed during the interview; and then faithfully reporting the interview results without bias or preconception.

The question of ''motive'' has often entered the public discussion when the validity of refugee reports is debated. Some would ask whether the refugee might not have some ulterior purpose in providing POW/MIA information. Certainly, most refugees are under stressful conditions, having recently departed their homeland, perhaps never to return or never to see loved ones again. They are desperate to be accepted for resettlement but threatened with possible rejection. It is quite conceivable that such persons, in their eagerness to please or to call their plight to the attention of American authorities, might fabricate stories they think will interest the Americans. Indeed, there is no negative incentive or penalty incurred, even if it could be without doubt proven that the refugee is lying. Interviewers have always taken the position that there can be no linkage between providing

POW/MIA information, whether truthful or not, and the refugee's opportunity for resettlement. If ever the refugees were to perceive a connection and their resettlement was at risk, surely the flow of possibly vital information would stop. Consequently, interviewers have duly noted the information provided, while accepting that there will be a certain percentage of fabrication, and have relied on the talent of the trained and experienced JCRC and DIA analysts to sort out fact from fiction.

THE INFORMATION PROVES USEFUL

Has the still on-going refugee interview activity proved worthwhile after well over a decade of effort? What conclusions can be drawn? Has anything of value been learned? Has the information analysis apparatus simply been clogged up by thousands and thousands of conjured-up stories?

Certainly no knowledgeable person would claim that everything reported as a result of refugee interviews is true, or even useful for that matter. There has been no spectacular breakthrough in the number of casualties resolved as a result of information acquired during the interview process. Much of what has been reported is still open to further analysis, since many of the reports can neither be proved nor disproved. The analysts at this point can only say that in many instances the information cannot be correlated to any known case of missing Americans.

Over the years, however, the information gleaned from refugees in this way has added immeasurably to US government knowledge of what took place during the war, and what fate befell a number of those individuals who were unaccounted for. One such example is the case of Navy Lieutenant Commander John Graf who ejected from his reconnaissance aircraft on 15 November 1969 over former Vinh Binh province, 80 miles south of Saigon. Numerous reports were received that related his capture by the Viet Cong and subsequent drowning during an attempt to escape by swimming a nearby river. His body was later recovered by the VC and buried along the river bank. More recent reports reveal that the gravesite has been eroded away by the annual river floods. We have learned of specific grave site locations from people who lived in the war zones and who have recounted their experiences in finding and burying the remains of Americans left behind after battles. From those who have witnessed the shootdown of American aircraft, we have sometimes learned the true fate of the crewmen.

Others who have reported their personal observations of persons in Vietnam whom they believe to be Americans living freely or held in varying degrees of captivity, have contributed to our knowledge of a number of known cases of Americans who were in Vietnam. Through refugee reports, for example. We learned of the incarceration and eventual death in Saigon's Chi Hoa Prison of Mr. Tucker Gougelmann, an American civilian trapped in Saigon at the time of the 1975 evacuation. Unfortunately, many gaps still exist in our knowledge; many of the reports that still remain uncorrelated, unexplained, unconfirmed, or undenied serve only to further frustrate the efforts to resolve the issue.

Perhaps among the most useful information gathered from the refugee interview program is that which contributes to our understanding of events previously reported but not understood at the time. The example of rumors of an escaped American pilot near Hanoi was cited earlier. Another example demonstrates how the acquisition of one small piece of new information can quickly lead to the resolution of numerous previously uncorrelated reports: Puzzling refugee reports had alleged the sighting of an individual, either held captive or being moved from place to place, at various locations in the southern Vietnam delta region following the communist takeover of Saigon in 1975. The refugees variously described the man as a Frenchman, a Belgian, or an American. Other intriguing reports alleged that this individual may have died and been interred near a prison at Can Tho.

Fortuitously, in mid-1981, a Vietnamese lady wrote from Saigon to the American embassy in Bangkok that she had heard the American government was interested in information about missing Americans. She related a story about her husband, an American civilian of ethnic French background born in Great Britain. Her husband had secretly returned to Vietnam from the United States following the 1975 collapse of South Vietnam, she wrote, with the intention of gaining the release of his wife and their two small children. Subsequently, he had been arrested, she said, by Vietnamese authorities of the new communist government and detained at a prison facility at Can Tho. Thereafter she heard reports, which she was unable to confirm, that her husband had died. The letter contained sufficient information to positively identify her husband and to permit a follow-up investigation with her husband's relatives in the United States. Further investigation and the attendant analysis confirmed the wife's information and her husband's unfortunate death while in captivity at Can Tho.

Though this did not turn out to be a prisoner-of-war case, the investigation had nevertheless led to the resolution of a large number of previously uncorrelated and inexplicable refugee reports. (The remains of Mr. Jean Lecornec, the American in this case, were repatriated to US custody by Vietnamese authorities in Hanoi on 14 August 1985, almost precisely ten years after Lecornec's death, most likely from the effects of dysentery contracted while incarcerated in a camp near Can Tho.)

In summary, a number of general conclusions can be drawn from the information-gathering effort. First, sufficient interviews have been conducted with Vietnamese government workers to confirm what plain logic and previously acquired information also tells us: There is overwhelming evidence that the Indochinese governments, at some location within their bureaucracies, have considerable knowledge of the fate of missing Americans. This information has not been readily made available. This is due partly to deliberate design on the part of the Vietnamese government, but to a lesser degree may also be a reflection of the difficulty associated with retrieving this information from written records or personal memories after the lengthy passage of time.

Second, a number of provable, true, and extremely useful reports have surfaced during refugee interviews, some of which would never have been uncovered by any other means, even with complete cooperation and disclosure of information by Indochinese officials. This situation is understandable and logical, given the tendency of people in the countryside to harbor a basic distrust of their own government officials, and their reluctance to report to these officials specific casualty-related information which they have discovered on their own.

Third, refugee interviews have helped the US authorities to amass a base of background information and data against which to evaluate the accuracy or truth of any new reports. This information may not necessarily pertain directly to the MIA topic, but can be very useful, say, in identifing specific places or time periods. For example, a concerted effort was made to piece together an extremely detailed and complete history of the evolution of the "re-education" camp system in northern Vietnam. Then, by having a former camp inmate sketch the layout of the camp in which he had been incarcerated, analysts were able to not only confirm which camp he was held in, but also determine the period of time he was there. This knowledge, in turn, could then be used to pinpoint the time and place of sightings of alleged Americans that he reported.

A great deal of information has been gathered about the presence in Vietnam, at various times after 1975, of a number of American personnel. It must be understood however, that so far there is not yet any confirming information regarding individuals who could be termed prisoners of war. Unbeknown to much of the American public there was no shortage of individuals, many of them Americans, who were candidates for having been sighted in Vietnam following the supposed complete US departure at the end of April 1975. Individuals known to have been present at one time or other include a handful of

Americans captured by North Vietnamese forces during their final push toward conquest of the South. This group included missionaries, civilian workers, and several United States government employees. A number of other Americans willingly or inadvertently got left behind during the evacuation from Saigon. In addition, information has been gathered on several Americans who lived in the Vietnamese countryside, and some who ended up in Vietnamese jails for various infractions. Indeed, there remains to be written an interesting collection of true tales, both humorous and tragic, of assorted American adventurers, do-gooders, criminals, and a few just plain folks, who for various periods of time and under mixed circumstances, resided (or still reside) within the Vietnamese borders.

Another significant benefit of the information gathering effort has been better knowledge of the policies pursued by Vietnam during and since the war in their handling of American casualties and remains. Such knowledge has helped United States officials fill voids in our understanding of exactly what took place on the battlefields in and over Southeast Asia. Refugee information became particularly useful with the advent of regular meetings between representatives of the United States and the Indochinese states, providing much-needed ammunition for these discussions on the subject of missing Americans.

When evaluating the results of the effort to acquire MIA-related information from refugees, one final factor must be considered. As information was gathered, analyzed, and correlated, it was inevitable that family members, congressmen, and the media would take note. Equally inevitable was the fact that, as more attention was focussed on the issue of the missing-in-action, pressure increased on all elements of the US government to *do* something toward resolving the issue. Ironically, as this public pressure increased within the United States, other factors were coming into play that prevented any accelerated progress.

PROGRESS SLOWS

As noted earlier, after the visit by a Vietnamese delegation to the JCRC and CIL in Hawaii in July 1978 the SRV repatriated the remains of 11 American servicemen to a visiting group of congressmen the following month. While the pace of progress was painfully slow, both the visit and the repatriation signalled Vietnam's willingness to at least keep the door open to continued casualty resolution activity. A number of US officials expressed optimism that with the passage of time, cooperation could be enhanced and the pace could be speeded up.

Any such optimism proved to be premature, however, when the SRV invasion of Cambodia in late 1978 and early 1979 put a freeze on the already cool relations between Vietnam and the United States. As the Vietnamese army forces sped westward across Cambodia in pursuit of the Chinese-supported Khmer Rouge forces of Pol Pot, the Deputy Prime Minister of China, Deng Xiaoping, was on an official visit to Washington, DC and threatening to "teach Vietnam a lesson."

Within days of Deng's return to China, a force of nearly 300,000 Chinese troops invaded and sacked the northern provinces of Vietnam. Then, during the one month that the Chinese forces were on Vietnamese soil, the United States and China exchanged ambassadors for the first time and officially opened embassies in each others' country. The timing of these events, whether deliberate or not, was viewed by the Socialist Republic of Vietnam as an indication of continued US hostility toward Vietnam. At a time when the Vietnamese felt world opinion should favor their attacks against Pol Pot's genocidal Khmer Rouge regime, the United States had sided with Vietnam's historic enemy, China.

At the same time, another event took place that further cooled the atmosphere. Among the stream of boat refugees fleeing from northern Vietnam, one of particular interest was discovered in a refugee camp in Hong Kong. This refugee, an ethnic Chinese from Hanoi, had previously worked for the Hanoi City Directorate of Cemeteries until he and his family were expelled from the country during the continuing purge of Chinese residents in 1979. Interestingly, this man, referred to as a "mortician", revealed that in the conduct of his duties he had personally prepared or observed the remains of over 400 American servicemen. This was not a mortician in the same sense of the word that Americans would expect. Vietnamese burial customs do not normally include embalming of the bodies of the deceased. Consequently, remains which are buried in the traditional wooden coffin normally decompose within a relatively short time. It is customary, after a period of three to five years after the interment, to disinter the remains of the deceased (skeletonized by that time), to clean the bones, and to place them in a clay urn or box for reinterment in a family grave. This process of disinterring the skeletal remains, cleaning and treating them with chemicals to retard the growth of mold in the damp climate, and reinterring the remains was carried out by the Vietnamese mortician.

Following his discovery, the mortician was extensively debriefed, both in Hong Kong and later after his resettlement in the United States. By checking his technical expertise, and by comparing events and details of his activities and his participation in remains repatriations which he related to interviewers, his identity and credentials were confirmed. Any lingering doubt, if any had existed, was dispelled when the mortician was positively identified by the French liaison officer with whom he had previously worked years earlier in the course of repatriation of French remains from Vietnam, and when the mortician's face was identified in US photos taken during the March 1974 repatriation of American remains from Hanoi.

The question of the mortician's claim of having processed or seen over 400 United States remains in Hanoi was also addressed by DIA interviewers and analysts. This claim (except, perhaps, for the number) was also verified both by means of polygraph exams and by comparing technical details revealed by the mortician with actual remains already repatriated from Vietnam and identified by the Central Identification Laboratory. (In addition to his knowledge about American remains, the mortician also made claim to having sighted on several occasions after Operation Homecoming several caucasians whom he was told were American prisoners of war. These reports are still open and under investigation.)

In January 1980 a Congressional Delegation, led by Congressman Lester Wolff (D-NY) traveled to Hanoi. The delegation confronted officials there with the fact that the United States was aware that the SRV was, in effect, storing the remains of US servicemen. The delegation pressed the Vietnamese officials for an investigation and the speedy repatriation of these remains. The Vietnamese officials' reaction to this open confrontation was to emphatically and indignantly deny they had stockpiled any remains. The Vietnamese reiterated their position that any remains found by their citizenry would be promptly repatriated to the United States.

In July 1980, in the presence of a group of family members and media representatives, Congressman Wolff chaired hearings of the House Foreign Affairs Subcommittee on East Asian and Pacific Affairs at which time the Vietnamese mortician testified publicly regarding his knowledge of American remains held in SRV custody. As before, the Vietnamese again denied the charges, contending that they were fabrications maliciously spread by disgruntled ethnic Chinese refugees.

During 1979-1980, sporadic communication had continued between Vietnam and the United States. In addition to several congressional trips to Hanoi during this period, the return of Marine PFC Robert Garwood to US custody in March 1979 prompted a month of flurried exchanges. Also, though SRV officials had earlier agreed in principle to the idea of holding technical talks—discussion of individual cases—with US officials on specific matters relating to missing Americans, they did not permit such a meeting until late 1980 when two members of the JCRC Liaison Office in Bangkok were allowed to go to Hanoi. These talks, though polite, were generally unproductive and served only to establish a precedent for other technical talks which were to come later. Consequently, despite sporadic contacts during 1979 and 1980, little real progress was achieved. Relations between Vietnam and the United States were primarily influenced by US unhappiness with Vietnam's invasion and occupation of Cambodia, by Vietnam's equal unhappiness over the US "tilt" toward China at the same time, and the spate of negative media coverage prompted by US accusations of SRV "stockpiling" of American servicemen's remains. Not until early 1981 could slight progress resume on the issue of missing Americans.

THE REAGAN INHERITANCE

The abbreviated presidency of Gerald Ford, followed by the four years of Jimmy Carter's presidency were years of frustration and disappointment, both for the families of missing Americans, and for those who were charged with the responsibility to assist in resolving the issue. Both Presidents had expressed sincere sympathy, and lent moral support to the cause of determining the fate of those still lost. However, by their actions, both Presidents attempted to put the Vietnam era behind. They sought to bring this period of American history to an end, hoping to somehow tie up the messy loose ends into a neat package and smooth over the emotional scars which had resulted from the war.

This movement back toward "business as usual" left the family members unfulfilled. In their eyes, the same government which had sent their sons and husbands off to war was now reluctant to aggressively pursue the cause of determining what had happened to those who did not return. During the Ford years, the final report of a major Congressional Committee effort had recommended, in effect, that those still unaccounted for be declared killed in action. This same committee had also expressed very limited expectations of the possibility of recovering many remains. Carter, in turn, had moved strongly, though unsuccessfully, toward normalization of relations with Vietnam, without posing any preconditions of Vietnamese cooperation to resolve this sensitive issue.

Casualty resolution activity during the Carter era was marked in its later years by organizational difficulties. US government action on the MIA issue over the preceding years had generally been carried out through a loose cooperative effort between the Department of Defense and the Department of State. Defense understandably had the predominant interest simply because it was mainly personnel from DOD whose fate was under investigation. The key Defense Department action organizations (as opposed to policy organizations) were the Defense Intelligence Agency (DIA) and its elements throughout the world, plus the Joint Casualty Resolution Center (JCRC), and the Army's Central Identification Laboratory (CIL).

The Department of State also had an essential role to play primarily because the accounting effort, by its very nature, involved contacts with foreign governments and officials, the guiding of these contacts clearly being within the purview of the State Department. To a lesser extent, State was involved because of its responsibility to account for those other US citizens missing—rather more than 40 civilians—who were not members of the US military forces.

Theoretically, on the military side, policy guidance and direction came from the office of the Secretary of Defense, specifically from the Assistant Secretary of Defense for International Security Affairs. This guidance was then passed to the action elements within DOD via the Office of the Joint Chiefs of Staff (JCS), and thence downward through the chain of command. Similarly, requests for support, or reports and recommendations, would travel back up the chain of command. In the case of the JCRC, for example, the communication path would be from the Secretary of Defense through the JCS and downward to CINCPAC in Hawaii, and then to the JCRC. While this arrangement is the normal military way of doing things, it created considerable problems.

The JCRC and the Central Identification Laboratory, the two elements working on the "cutting edge" of all casualty resolution activity, both had absolutely no other purpose for existence, and no other collateral mission or responsibilities competed for their attention. This was not the case for each and every other organizational layer or element above the JCRC and the CIL in their respective chains of command. For these higher-level organizations, dealing with the topic of casualty resolution was, at best, a part-time job, something to be carried out along with the multitude of other competing tasks that faced the headquarters staffer or action officer each day. This situation hindered not only the acquisition and allocation of resources, but also the free flow of ideas and suggestions between the "doers" in the field and the policymakers in Washington, DC.

As the Carter administration came to a close, there was no staunch organizational "advocate" in Washington, DC for the continuation of the casualty resolution task. Increasingly, the question being asked was, "How soon can we shut down this effort?" Within an environment characterized by such a question, one might understand how requests from JCRC for increases in travel funds, or for additional personnel with specialized talent, for example, were not always looked on kindly by those who themselves were being asked to trim both funds and manpower in their own activities. Similarly, ideas and suggestions from the field for getting on with the casualty resolution effort, which often involved a closer and cooperative arrangement with counterpart personnel from the communist-dominated Indochinese governments, were not always passed upward with great enthusiasm.

REORGANIZING FOR MORE EFFECTIVE ACTION

President Reagan came into office predisposed to take more aggressive action on the resolution of American casualties. He had long held a personal interest in this issue and he often recalled in speeches his earlier days as Governor of California when he and Mrs. Reagan had first met with members of the League of Families and had later hosted a party for a large number of the returned POWs in 1973.

Early in the Reagan presidency action was taken to formulate a specific strategy to deal with the MIA issue in a more systematic and realistic manner. Among the elements of this strategy was a major effort to increase public knowledge of the MIA issue. As a consequence of several years of relative inactivity and little publicity, the American people generally had little knowledge that a problem still existed. More important still was the need to change the apparent perception of Vietnamese and Lao government officials whose actions seemed to indicate a belief that the issue was of little importance to America and would likely fade away given enough time.

Consequently, media contacts were increased to provide press representatives with factual information and the opportunity to address questions to government officials involved in the issue. The topic of missing Americans found its way into policy statements and major speeches delivered by the newly-elected President, his Secretaries of Defense and State, and numerous other government officials. The proclamation by the President of a National POW/MIA Recognition Day became an annual event, and the day was marked by special ceremonies, speeches, and other appropriate events sponsored in cooperation with the National League of Families.

Closer cooperation with the National League of Families became another element of the government's strategy. Whereas an adversarial relationship had previously existed between the government and the League, effort was now being made to consider more carefully the ideas and positions of the family members as expressed through the League. In a major policy change, individual case files were declassified and made available to family members for their inspection. In a further effort to draw closer to the families, new emphasis was given to the individual Service casualty offices, whose responsibility it was to maintain contact with the next-of-kin of those missing and to advise them individually of any activity on their particular case. The Department of Defense began publishing a ''Next-of Kin Newsletter'' for the purpose of keeping family members informed of current governmental activity and any other events which impacted on efforts to resolve the issue. At the same time, security access was granted by the DIA to the Executive Director of the League of Families in order that the Director could be briefed and kept abreast of any classified matters which could not be disseminated in a general manner throughout the entire League membership. In an unusual step, the Executive Director of the League was accepted as a full and regularly participating member of the government decision-making apparatus involving MIA matters.

Though the MIA issue had always enjoyed considerable attention from the intelligence community, action was initiated to once again heighten the priority and effectiveness of the intelligence effort devoted to this issue. The need for both overt and covert collection of information was stressed to intelligence entities throughout the world. Additional assets in the form of manpower and technical expertise were added, particularly in the Defense Intelligence Agency which had the key responsibility for collection and analysis of information on this issue. Other military and civilian intelligence organizations were also directed to increase their emphasis and attention to the matter.

The renewal and heightening of diplomatic activity and bilateral contacts also became another element of the Reagan strategy for attacking the MIA problem. After a shaky start, high-level policy contact was established with the Vietnamese government in early 1982 when then Deputy Assistant Secretary of Defense Richard Armitage led a small delegation to Hanoi to once again point out the mutual benefits which could accrue with renewed cooperation. While the discussions were termed ''candid but cordial,'' Vietnamese officials used the opportunity to make clear their view that there was a definite connection between their cooperation on the MIA issue and the US attitude and posture toward Vietnam.[3] SRV officials also accepted an earlier-tendered invitation to again send a delegation of experts for consultations in Hawaii with JCRC and CIL officials. (This visit later took place during the month of August.) At the same time, efforts to reemphasize the MIA issue with the Lao government through the American Embassy in Vientiane met with only minimal success.

In addition to these direct contacts with the Indochinese governments, diplomatic approaches were made to others who might be in a position to influence or encourage movement by the Indochinese states. Soon after assuming the duties of Secretary of State in mid-1982, George Shultz made personal approaches to the heads of the ASEAN countries (Indonesia, Malaysia, the Philippines, Singapore, and Thailand, at that time) requesting their support for US efforts and suggesting they use their influence to encourage added cooperation. Close allies and friends of the Indochinese states were also approached in a similar vein.

Back on the domestic front, the Reagan administration sought, and immediately received, bipartisan support for its efforts to bring added attention and emphasis to the MIA issue. Within the Congress, a special House POW/MIA Task Force was created to oversee the government effort. From the time of its inception the appointed Task Force Chairman has been a member of the minority party of the House of Representatives, indicative of the bipartisan support directed toward the MIA issue.

While formulation of an interlocking strategy for addressing the complexities of the MIA issue constituted a major forward step in the casualty resolution process, several organizational steps needed to be taken to overcome the previous drift in guidance of the overall US effort. Though the Defense Department was the executive agent for the Administration regarding the MIA issue, many other governmental entities also had an important part to play.

To bring order and to assure that each "player" was working in harmony with the overall strategy, a POW/MIA Interagency Group (IAG) was created. Membership included representatives from both the State and Defense Departments, the National Security Council staff, the Joint Chiefs of Staff, the Defense Intelligence Agency, the National League of Families, and from relevant committees of the House and Senate.[4] While the IAG was chaired by the State Department representative, the representative from the National Security Council staff monitored the diverse aspects of all governmental MIA-related activity on a daily basis to assure a coherent effort. With the creation of the IAG in 1982, the US government had for the first time a single unified group which could formulate policy, assess on-going efforts, evaluate and discuss new initiatives, and generally assure that the impact on the MIA issue was considered when various government actions were contemplated.

The impact of the formulation of a unified strategy for addressing the MIA issue, the establishment of the IAG, and the resultant focusing of attention on this issue, cannot be overstated. It was these actions which brought order to what had previously been a piecemeal effort and, even more significant for the families and for those who were daily involved in the issue, there finally existed in Washington, DC, a sense of advocacy for proceeding with the mission of resolving the fate of those still missing. President Reagan himself signalled this renewed government emphasis during a speech delivered to a gathering sponsored by the National League of Families on 28 January 1983. Stressing the goals of gaining release for any prisoners, achieving the fullest possible accounting of the missing, and seeking repatriation of the remains of those killed, he assured the family members that after many years of malaise, the government's attention and assets were now fully focussed on this issue. "The government bureaucracy now understands that these goals are the highest national priority," he said.[5]

NOTES

1. This comment was written in a note sent between Bangkok-based refugee officers on 9 November 1978 at a time when concerted efforts were being made by JCRC to take a more active stance and to emphasize and streamline the program to interview refugees for any POW/MIA information which they might possess. In defense of the note-writer, the feelings expressed were generally in accord with State Department policy which at that time also opposed the active solicitation of information from the refugees in the camps. State Department message 78 STATE 112448, DTG 031600Z MAY 78, made reference to this position when it stated, "We have in the past assured MIA relatives that US officials follow up PW/MIA reports from Indochina refugees whenever they come to our attention, but that we have refrained from aggressive de-briefings on this subject to avoid stimulating possibly false or exaggerated responses." This message announced no new policy in this regard, but went on only to ask field elements to ensure that a program existed to receive and report POW/MIA information brought to US officials' attention by the refugees.

2. Refugee departure statistics are quoted from an article published in the December 1979 issue of the *Department of State Bulletin* entitled "Refugees: An International Obligation," by Harry F. Young.

3. *CINCPAC Command History, 1982 (TS)*, vol. II, 16 September 1983, p. 376.

4. *POW-MIA Fact Book*, Department of Defense, July 1989, p. 3.

5. Quoted from the text, released by the White House Press Secretary, of an address delivered by President Reagan to the National League of Families at the Hyatt Regency Hotel in Crystal City, Virginia, on 28 January 1983.

4

PRIVATE INVOLVEMENT

THE NATIONAL LEAGUE OF FAMILIES

As one might expect, the US government is not the only entity involved in the efforts to determine the fate of those still missing and unaccounted for. Family members, out of their great personal concern for their loved ones, have involved themselves in various ways from the day of initial notification of the casualty incident. As noted earlier, family members traveled to Paris during the time of the US-Vietnamese negotiations in an effort to press for answers to their many questions. The commonality of interest among family members, coupled with their increased activism in the late 1960s, led to the eventual formalization of the group and their incorporation in May 1970 as the National League of Families of American Prisoners and Missing in Southeast Asia, generally abbreviated to the National League of Families.[1]

The early history of the League of Families was often characterized by a widely held adversarial position toward the US government. This position had developed from resentment toward the government's earlier desire that the families refrain from publicly discussing the MIA problem, along with the government's policy of keeping a low profile on the issue—a policy which the families equated with government inaction. Following the repatriation of prisoners during Operation Homecoming in early 1973, much resentment continued over the manner in which the government handled the status changes of the missing. Meanwhile, the League continued to press for additional attention to the plight of those still unaccounted for. Largely as a result of League pressure, Congressman Montgomery's House Select Committee on Missing Persons in Southeast Asia (see Chapter 2) was formed; however, the committee's conclusions and final report led only to additional controversy and alienation between the family members and the government. League hopes were once again buoyed by President Carter's early appointment of the Woodcock Commission to travel to Hanoi and Vientiane "to obtain the best possible accounting for the missing." The Commission's failure to achieve this lofty goal once again led to disillusionment on the part of the League members.

As the Carter administration continued to distance itself from the League during the administration's later years, the families became more and more vocal in their criticism of government actions. The League rightly claimed that the United States was slow in organizing to conduct interviews with the flood of refugees from Indochina in 1978 and 1979. Largely out of frustration, the League began to take initiatives on its own which, in the long run, were counterproductive to the overall effort.

The League encouraged placement of advertisements in various publications which found their way to the refugee camps in Southeast Asia. These solicited information about missing Americans, offering rewards and implying resettlement assistance for any such information. At a time when personnel from both the Defense Intelligence Agency and the Joint Casualty Resolution Center were attempting to expand the refugee interview program, the effect of these ads was to deter refugees from confiding their information to government interviewers. In a number of instances, for example, leads were generated as a result of the ads and were then passed by the League to the DIA for follow-up contact and interview in the refugee camps. When a US official later made contact in the camp to conduct a detailed interview, the refugee would first inquire about his promised reward.

League activity also included subsidizing several private individuals to search for MIA information in Asia. There was even a brief flirtation by the League with the idea of privately inspired POW rescue attempts. One of the most counterproductive efforts was instigated by a League-sponsored individual who encouraged the direct involvement of Laotian resistance fighters in the recovery of American remains from crashsites in Laos. Unfortunately, this involvement led to a spate of false reports, a rise in attempts by Lao resistance personnel to barter for remains, and the destruction of possibly useful evidence at crashsites as well as the dispersal of potentially identifiable human remains.

Fortunately, the frustration which had driven the League to involve itself in these activities eventually eased as the US government once again focussed its attention on the MIA issue in 1981 and 1982. In September 1982, with the US government's blessing and encouragement, a four-person delegation from the National League of Families traveled to Vientiane and Hanoi to meet directly with Lao and Vietnamese officials to make known the views of the families which they represented. This journey, the first by a League delegation to Hanoi, also included side-trips in Laos to visit two aircraft crashsites. Undoubtedly there were educational benefits for both sides as a result of this trip: the League delegation learned firsthand about some of the difficulties encountered when dealing with Indochinese officials and of the complexities of crashsite investigations, while the Indochinese officials learned about the depth of feeling of the families and their desire to resolve the MIA issue.

Tensions between the US government and the League of Families continued to ease with the passage of time as communication between the two entities improved. After the decision was made by the DIA in November 1979 to grant the Executive Director of the

League access to classified information, there was marked improvement in this relationship. Later on, with the creation of the Interagency Group (IAG) and the inclusion of the League Executive Director as a full member of this body, the relationship completed its evolution from one of hostility toward one of cooperation. It must be pointed out that "cooperation" implied only that the League and the government would work together toward a common goal. It did not, and does not, imply complete agreement. It is to be expected that the League, representing the special interests of the family members of the missing, would not always be in one hundred percent agreement with the US government whose actions must at times be dictated by larger national interests. Further, though there is agreement on the ultimate goal of achieving the fullest possible accounting of those still missing, differences still arise on how to attain that goal.

Nevertheless, as the League drew closer to the government, its influence widened. The League's views were increasingly sought, not only by the administration, but also by the legislative committees and subcommittees which deliberated on matters of US interest in Asia. In recent years the Executive Director of the League of Families has been called upon innumerable times to present testimony to Congress and to elaborate on League positions. The Director has also been included as a full-fledged member of government delegations which have dealt with Indochinese officials, both in Asia and at the United Nations Headquarters in New York, whenever matters of League interest were to be discussed.

There is no question that the increased cooperation between the League of Families and the government has been beneficial. The League's views are now heard, and are taken into consideration when plans are made and actions are contemplated. Equally important, this cooperation, openly advertised, has sent a significant signal to the Indochinese governments that both the US government and the families share common views and goals. This, in turn, has negated any attempts by the Indochinese governments to drive a wedge between the families and their government.

The US government's unusual quasi-official relationship with the League has also proved useful in strategic matters. There are times, for example, when it is useful for the Executive Director of the League to say things to Vietnamese officials, with whom we have no diplomatic relations, which cannot be said directly by American officials. This arrangement is a two-way street; it permits the Vietnamese to pass subtle messages through the League Director when it would be awkward or diplomatically inappropriate to pass them directly to the US government. In this way, unofficial communication with the Vietnamese government via the League has opened an additional and useful channel for the exchange of views between the two countries.

Critics of the League of Families, of which there indeed is no shortage, contend that the League has been co-opted by the US government and, therefore, has compromised its own independence and lost its credibility. Other critics have expressed concern about the precedent of government allying itself so closely with what is, essentially, a private non-governmental lobbying organization. What would be the result, they ask, if other such organizations were formed which also claimed to represent a substantial number of the family members of the missing? Would the US government draw equally close to them? And would the government also take into account any other organization's views and suggestions, and incorporate them into the decision-making process to plot the course of future efforts? Whether or not there is any reason for concern over this possible precedent, or any validity in the contention that the League has lost its effectiveness because of this association, all indications are that the symbiotic relationship between the League and the US government has been beneficial, on balance, both to the family members and to those in the government charged with carrying out the mission of accounting for those still missing.

The real value of the League, however, can be realized when one contemplates what would have been the ultimate course of events had the League never existed.

One could pose a convincing argument that the US government would not have devoted the effort and resources to resolving the resolution of the MIA issue had it not been pushed so aggressively by the League. This is not to imply that the government lacked concern for the issue, and for the family members who still await an answer to their uncertainty. This is only an acknowledgement that, following a war, the military has generally attempted to "wrap things up" and get on with business as usual. Indeed, this theme was often heard during the late 1970s from government officials who would have eliminated the JCRC and let the casualty resolution mission revert to the State Department for negotiation purposes, and to the Army's Graves Registration units for recovery and repatriation of remains. One can perhaps envision how the Department of Defense, as a bureaucracy, could adopt the pragmatic attitude that in time of war soldiers get killed, incinerated, blown to bits, and lost, and in many cases we will never know what happened to the individual. To the League of Families must go the credit for inspiring the bureaucracy to try harder.

OTHER MIA INTEREST GROUPS

A number of other groups also share an interest in the MIA issue. Among these groups are the traditional veterans organizations such as the Veterans of Foreign Wars, the American Legion, the Disabled American Veterans and, of more recent vintage, the Vietnam Veterans of America. The interest of these and other such groups is fueled by their patriotism and their traditional support for issues related to the welfare of military personnel. Many other groups and associations have also picked up the POW/MIA banner and have been supportive, not only of the family members but also of the US government's efforts to resolve the issue. These cover the entire spectrum from the Medal of Honor Society and the Non-Commissioned Officers Association, for example, down to the local Boy Scout troops and the local high school current events class, with perhaps hundreds of groups in between.

While everyone is seemingly unanimous in their support to resolve the issue of missing Americans, not all groups share the belief that the US government is pursuing the task with sufficient enthusiasm. In more recent years, a number of other organizations have sprung up which have as a common denominator their strong belief that the government is not only insufficiently active on the issue, but also duplicitous in its relations with the family members. The membership of some of these groups includes, in addition to interested citizens, a number of family members, many of whom are former members of the League of Families who believe that the League has been co-opted by the government and no longer represents their best interests. Unfortunately, the relationship between a few of these "splinter groups" and the League of Families has at times taken on an extremely adversarial character. This has been manifested, for example, in hostile diatribes published in their respective newsletters, and by assorted disruptive activities. In one instance, a disgruntled group attempted the forceful takeover of the national offices of the League of Families in Washington, DC, in March 1987.

Nor have these groups reserved their hostility for the League alone. Character attacks and other forms of harassment have been directed against a number of government officials who have been associated with resolving the MIA issue over the years. While much of this hostility could be attributed to understandable frustration over the slow pace of progress, some also must be attributed to outright mean-spiritedness and a self-serving desire for publicity.

Even more reprehensible, however, are the activities of a few groups who have seized upon the MIA issue as a means to make money. Characteristically, these groups have wrapped themselves in the cloak of humanitarianism, claiming their goal in life is to seek information

about missing Americans, or to rescue American servicemen they "know" with absolute certainty are still held
in captivity. When confronted with a request for funds to
support such activity, what donor could object to such a
high-minded endeavor? These fund-raising groups, some
using the most modern and sophisticated techniques developed by the mail solicitation industry, have managed
to raise hundreds of thousands of dollars yearly for questionable activity and equally questionable results, and all
without the burden of financial accountability. Unfortunately, the ones hit hardest by this combination of emotional appeal and implied promise of favorable outcome
are often those who can least afford to contribute, either
emotionally or financially: the relatives and friends of
those who are still missing.

Many of the fund raising letters imply that their organization is on the brink of rescuing an American prisoner of war, and that the prisoner will die unless the
recipient of the letter sends money immediately. Typical
of these appeals are the following, quoted from the solicitation letters of three different groups:

> We're close to making contact with an American
> POW who has been alone since his fellow prisoner
> died of natural causes less than a year ago. That
> effort could fail for lack of funds. Please be as gener-
> ous as you can as soon as you can. Thank you.[2]

> I'm exhausted. I'm broke. And, I'm reaching the end of
> my rope. But, I believe we are very, very close to getting
> our first POW out. I can't give you any more details.
> But you may wake up tomorrow morning and hear that
> the first American POW has been rescued. We are that
> close![3]

> But whatever you can send today in the enclosed envelope
> to help, you may rest assured that you have done your
> part to restore America's honor. I promise to tell all of
> our hostages, when they are finally freed, of the vital role
> you played in their release. I wish you would write a

brief note on the enclosed donation card, which I will
personally hand to the first man to regain his freedom.[4]

The Defense Intelligence Agency has expended considerable time and effort investigating claims made by
various groups which are soliciting funds on the POW/
MIA issue. According to a 1987 study conducted by DIA
at the request of Congressman Stephen Solarz of the
House Subcommittee on Asian and Pacific Affairs of the
House Committee on Foreign Affairs, DIA found that
many of the fund-raising letters included "little or no
substantive data which would lend itself to serious intelligence analysis, but instead are rambling discourses filled
with inflammatory rhetoric." Based on a detailed analysis of the statements and the accompanying "facts" cited
in support of these statements, DIA concluded that these
organizations were basing their fund appeals on claims
which were, at best, highly suspicious, and in many instances, demonstrably false. DIA also observed that "it
is noteworthy that for all their 'proof' and the untold
millions of dollars raised, none of these groups or individuals have yet to furnish even the slightest shred of evidence of POWs, much less secure the return of a living
American captive."[5]

In addition to DIA, the League of Families also went
on record as opposing the activities of these groups. The
League noted that in some instances family members had
been contacted directly by individuals claiming to have
proof that particular Americans were still alive in captivity, yet offering no supporting evidence. Unfortunately,
in spite of League condemnation and these groups' lack
of success in making a contribution toward resolving the
MIA issue, their fund-raising activities continue.

RISE OF THE "RAMBOS"

The Reagan administration's emphasis on wider
publicty for the MIA issue brought a new awareness of

this topic to the American public. With this new awareness came another disruptive phenomena, the private rescue efforts. Regrettably, added emphasis and an element
of public sympathy for such activity was inspired by movies such as *Rambo* and others of the same genre. As with
many aspects of the MIA issue, emotionalism occasionally prevails over logic, and there is ample sympathy for
the idea of "overcoming the hated enemy" to rescue any-
one who may still be held captive. The premises apparently shared by those who would contemplate such
activity are first, that conclusive proof of the existence of
Americans still held captive is available, second, the US
government is either unwilling or unable to rescue them,
and third, an unofficial private foray would be successful
in locating and freeing the captives. Indeed, there has
been no shortage of reports of Americans still held in
captivity. Seldom did the interviewers in JCRC visit a
refugee camp without receiving several reports of alleged
Americans in varying degrees of captivity. Public knowledge of such reports has become widespread, and these
reports undoubtedly inspire much of the private rescue
talk and activity.

Not widely known, however, are the analyses of these
reports. Of the thousands of sighting reports received
over the past decade, nearly all have been resolved. Many
have been correlated to known cases of individuals who
were at one time in Indochina but who later departed,
such as released POWs, foreign yachtsmen captured off-
shore, missionaries, persons who remained in Vietnam
following the April 1975 evacuation, and so on. Some of
the sightings of alleged Americans have been correlated to
individuals with distinctly Caucasian features, who were
known to work or reside in Vietnam. For example, a man
nicknamed "Tony Hai" lives in Ho Chi Minh City; his
full-bearded face easily passes for that of an American.
Other segments of the live sighting reports, after detailed
analysis, have been judged to be untrue.

Because of the remaining relatively small number of
reports which have not yet been resolved—and which are
still undergoing extensive investigation and analysis—the

Vietnamese citizen Tran Huu Hai (also known as "Tony" Hai) is often mistaken for an American still living in Vietnam.

US government has taken the prudent position that it does not rule out the possibility that American POWs may still be held against their will. The unhappy truth, however, is that there still exists no conclusive proof of American POWs still held captive in Indochina. (For the sake of clarity, though, it must be noted that there is very strong evidence of American law-breakers presently held in Indochinese jails as a consequence of their illicit drug activity.)

Therefore, the claims of sure knowledge of the existence of American captives by the so-called "Rambos", intent on charging into the Southeast Asian jungles to conduct a rescue, have yet to be proved. While these individuals have often publicly declared that they possess sure proof of American captives, no one has yet produced this evidence. Even retired Army Lieutenant Colonel "Bo" Gritz, perhaps the most charismatic and famous of those who have either participated in or advocated private rescue forays, admitted he had no hard evidence of American captives after his abortive rescue treks into Laos in 1983.[6]

Based on some of the amazing antics of those individuals and groups advocating private forays in search of American prisoners, it is sometimes difficult to believe they are truly serious. Though espousing the goal of freeing alleged captives, an effort which one would ordinarily expect to be shrouded in secrecy, in actuality these so-called rescue forays usually have been accompanied with much self-generated media hype.

"Bo" Gritz, during an earlier period of team training in Florida in preparation for a "clandestine" journey into Laos, invited at least one reporter as a member of the group. Later, following his arrest in Thailand at the conclusion of an abortive rescue foray, Gritz enthusiastically granted interviews to the TV and print media in a circus-like atmosphere at the Nakhon Phanom Provincial jail. Perhaps Admiral A. G. Paulson of DIA said it best during testimony on 22 March 1983 before the Asian and Pacific Affairs Subcommittee of the House Foreign

Affairs Committee when he stated regarding Gritz' activities:

> These efforts have seemed like a parody, a caricature of the clandestine operation, the 'surgical penetration' he purports to be capable of mounting. Concerning his reputation as a soldier, his activities have been inexplicable from an intelligence point of view. At the onset, he is confronted with an apparently unsolvable dilemma, a requirement to solicit funds publicly and still keep his intentions private. Beyond this, he has been incapable of surrounding himself with associates who remain loyal to him or the purpose of keeping his intended operations undisclosed. As a final contradiction in clandestine operations, it seems he always keeps certain members of the media informed of his activity and intentions. . . . This exposure obviously is incongruent with his stated purpose to conduct undetected operations. . . . If Mr. Gritz truly believes that live Americans are being held, it must have occurred to him, as it does to us or any sensible person, that the publicity associated with his activity cannot but have a deleterious effect on any prisoner who may be still held in Southeast Asia.[7]

Gritz, however, is not the only one to involve himself in alleged forays into Indochina, or to claim a monopoly on patriotism and fervor over the issue of missing Americans. Other individuals and groups have periodically surfaced and made claims, either to having gone into Laos personally to search for missing Americans, or to be sponsoring such a foray by others—usually indigenous Lao resistance fighters. Most assuredly some of these claims are false, and are made for purposes of personal bravado or garnering credibility for fund-raising activities. One American citizen activist who has been heavily involved in fund solicitation, for example, made the unlikely claim to the JCRC Liaison Officer in Bangkok that he personally had trekked undetected across the entire breadth of the panhandle of southern Laos from the Mekong River to the border with Vietnam, allegedly in search of MIAs. As proof of this feat, he showed a photograph which he claimed to have taken himself, and which supposedly depicted the Highway 9 boundary marker at the border between the countries of Laos and Vietnam. Significantly, however, even more than the fact that his age and portliness pointed toward the unlikelihood he could withstand the physical rigors of such an undertaking, when questioned he was totally unable to elaborate in a consistent manner regarding any aspect of the trip details.

Though the motives of many individuals actively involved in private escapades are suspect, the emotional appeal of such activity is understandable. Nevertheless, the end result has been extremely counterproductive and has hindered overall US efforts to address the MIA problem. Experience has shown that invariably those who embark on these activities are operating on bad or non-existent intelligence and have virtually no chance for success, "*Rambo*" movies notwithstanding. As a further consideration, if there should happen to be prisoners held, word of possible rescue efforts would certainly promote additional caution on the part of the captors, and could ultimately prompt the elimination of any prisoners.

On the diplomatic front, the communist governments of the Indochinese states, always paranoid and particularly willing to believe the United States is intent on overthrowing their regimes, have seized upon these private forays, whether actually carried out or only threatened, as evidence of US ill will toward them. In their society, where governmental control over the individual citizen is so complete, they find it difficult to comprehend that a US citizen could conduct a foray on his own volition without the US government both condoning and sponsoring it. Further, to them it is unimaginable that the US government is relatively powerless to halt this activity. Consequently, when private forays by American citizens have resulted in accusations that the United

States is sponsoring raids into their sovereign territory, US denials have generally fallen on deaf ears.

One such example occurred in mid-February 1983. After years of effort by the American embassy in Vientiane, the Lao government for the first time had finally agreed to allow personnel from the JCRC and the Central Identification Laboratory to come to Vientiane and discuss some of the technical aspects of casualty resolution activities which were contemplated in Laos. As the talks began in Vientiane, the front page of *The Bangkok Post* carried a story of an on-going raid into Laos by American citizens allegedly intent on finding prisoners of war. The Lao officials, red with anger, heatedly accused the visiting delegation of complicity in violating the territory of Laos, and abruptly broke off the talks. The delegation was forced to depart without having achieved any positive results, essentially squandering the hard-won agreement to meet.

EFFORTS OF UNTRAINED AMATEURS

Another form of unhelpful private activity involves the attempted recovery of the remains of American servicemen. In a few instances, American citizens have themselves participated in this activity; however, more often they have promoted involvement on the part of others such as indigenous "resistance fighters" or refugees. Indeed it may be possible to resolve a very small number of cases by covertly dispatching someone into remote areas to recover skeletal remains. The US government has taken the position, however, that in order to address the larger number of cases, government-to-government cooperation is essential. The rationale for this position is more than simply political; it is based on very pragmatic factors.

Experience has shown that more harm than good can result from the efforts of untrained amateurs. The proper recovery of skeletal remains is not unlike the science of archeology. Care must be taken so that evidence and essential portions such as teeth or bone fragments, are not overlooked. These are vitally important to the physical anthropologists when making their identification. Further, the entire effort must be carefully documented and other secondary evidence noted, such as aircraft or engine serial numbers, weapons or personal effects, and the exact site location. Each final identification made by the laboratory must withstand legal scrutiny, and this requirement imposes strict conditions on how the remains and evidence are handled and accounted for. None of these sensitivities are taken into consideration when untrained individuals rummage through a grave site or crashsite in an attempt to recover identifiable remains. Not only is identification of any recovered remains put in jeopardy, amateur efforts will quite likely render the site useless to the trained lab experts who might later have the opportunity to properly excavate the same site.

Private non-governmental activity has also led to the problem, increasingly evident with time, of buying and selling remains. As American citizens have solicited (and paid) indigenous personnel to assist in covert remains-recovery efforts, they have implicitly placed a monetary value on these remains. As word spread, a whole new class of entrepreneurs sprang up in Southeast Asia among the refugees and "resistance fighters." As unseemly as this may appear, JCRC interviewers in Thailand and other refugee camps throughout Asia have been bombarded with offers of alleged remains of American servicemen, usually in exchange for money, material assistance for resistance efforts, or for priority treatment in refugee resettlement. The ultimate result of this phenomenon is the destruction and loss of evidence and remains as they are divided and subdivided as a form of "trading stock." The obliteration of grave and crashsites will likely render these cases unresolvable.

A secondary phenomenon is the glut of reports, nicknamed "dog tag" reports, which have been received, usually from fleeing Vietnamese refugees or from travelers to Vietnam. Typically, a refugee will present an interviewer with a bone fragment with the explanation that this is a portion of the remains of an American who was killed, and that the rest of the remains are being held by someone still in Vietnam. As further "proof," the refugee will provide either a rubbing of a serviceman's embossed metal "dog tag," or will provide this same information copied in a "dog tag" format, i.e., name, service number, blood type, and religion, with slight variations depending on the particular branch of service. Often this information and the remains have been received second or third-hand by the refugee, who therefore becomes an unwitting accomplice in the passing of information which is most often fallacious.

By 10 December 1991, the DIA had recorded 6,591 "dog tag" reports which included the names of 5,191 individual servicemen. Analysis of these reports showed that 91 percent of the "dog tag" names were those, not of casualties, but of Americans who returned home alive following their tours of duty in Vietnam. Another 6 percent of those named were killed in Vietnam, but their remains were recovered at the time of their deaths and were immediately repatriated back to the United States. Only 3 percent of the names were those of persons who are still unaccounted for. As can be seen from the number of reports and names, identical "dog tag" information is often provided by multiple sources, each of whom mistakenly believes he or she has provided unique information. Most often, the small fragments of remains which accompany these reports are insufficient for the Central Identification Laboratory to make any sort of conclusion, other than perhaps to determine that the remains are in fact of human origin, though this is not always the case.

The pervasiveness of this "dog tag" report phenomenon, coupled with analysis of its origin, has led the DIA to conclude that this is a managed disinformation effort, sponsored either by the Vietnamese government, by corrupt officials, or by other opportunists, and directed toward influencing the MIA resolution effort. Certainly this phenomena has caused much unproductive analytical effort. Additionally, as word has spread within Vietnam of the US government's interest in the recovery of the remains of missing Americans, fleeing refugees have more readily believed the false rumors of the necessity to provide "dog tag" information to American officials to gain acceptance for resettlement to the United States. As a consequence, many unsuspecting refugees have lost untold amounts of treasure buying remains fragments or other bogus information just before leaving Vietnam.

ATTEMPTS BY THE "CON ARTISTS"

The majority of people who have provided POW/MIA related information to the US government over the years have done so willingly, believing that most of what they are relating is true. It is not unusual, of course, for a bit of exaggeration to creep into a story, or for the storyteller to "embroider" his report with a few non-existent details to enhance the interest, or for him to assume a firsthand role when, in fact, he is reporting second or third-hand information. While such antics can be very troublesome to the analyst charged with attempting to substantiate or correlate the story, investigators have generally learned to recognize and cope with such tricks.

Of greater concern, however, are those instances where individuals have purposefully set out to deceive investigators by concocting totally false information. No discussion of private non-governmental activity would be complete without describing several of the more blatant efforts in this regard. The reasons for attempted fraud are not always obvious. In some of the more notable attempts, though, the motive appears to have been either to solicit material assistance for so-called resistance fighters, or to obtain money. In the examples described, the enticement or "commodity" used to get the US government's attention was either supposed proof of American prisoners or other "certain" information about the same.

In September 1985, American officials obtained an interesting photograph from a Lao resistance supporter

Peace Corps worker Greg Kamm, who was misrepresented as an American POW by unscrupulous individuals in Thailand. Kamm's Lao friend was alleged to be his guard.

residing in Thailand. This photo showed a tall Caucasian young man, well-dressed and well-groomed, standing in a wooded and rustic setting which included a thatched house. Next to this young man was a shorter Asian male, also well-dressed and pleasant looking. According to the Lao resistance member, this photo, recently taken at a camp in Laos, depicted an American prisoner of war along with his guard, a communist Lao lieutenant colonel.

Though photo analysis strongly suggested that the subject was not likely to be an American prisoner, officials were duly obliged to investigate on the premise that the story could be true. By December 1985, the person in the photo was positively identified as Mr. Greg Kamm, a Peace Corps volunteer working in Thailand as an instructor in an up-country teachers' school. When contacted, the astonished Kamm explained that the photo had been taken during one of his many visits to Lao friends who lived in Thailand, and he identified the other man in the photograph as one of these friends. Kamm later was able to also confirm that the negative of the photo had been taken by another Lao who was closely associated with the Lao resistance. Meanwhile, as investigation into the identity of those in the photo was proceeding, other US officials were being contacted, occasionally through intermediaries, in attempts to solicit money for the alleged purpose of assisting the Lao resistance forces. The photo of Kamm, still being touted as a POW, was often displayed as "bait" to prompt US interest.

In one memorable instance, an American official was enticed to meet at a Bangkok hotel with a Thai businessman intermediary plus two accompanying Lao resistance supporters who had concocted a revised story of American prisoners. With all seriousness, the Lao resistance supporters presented a written proposal for their forces to rescue American prisoners which they "knew with absolute certainty" were being held captive in several locations in Laos. This proposal included the very carefully calculated cost of the rescue operation, including anticipated duration, manpower required, and expected level of casualties. The cost was to be slightly over 1.25 million dollars, with 10 percent to be paid in advance.

When proof of the existence of the captives was requested, once again the infamous "Greg Kamm" photo was brought out for inspection. This time, however, the photo had the face of the Asian "guard" cut out "since he was really a Lao resistance agent and needed to have his true identity protected." After hearing the complete story, and after questioning these gentlemen to "clarify" some of the details, the American official withdrew from his briefcase an exact copy of the photo, face intact, explained the realities of the photo, and suggested to the gentlemen that they had apparently been misled by their own informant, who had obviously tried to give them bad information. In the uneasy and embarrassing silence that followed, the official excused himself and left the red-faced "businessmen" to reflect among themselves.

Not all scams are as straightforward and obviously false as those described above; some are more serpentine and elaborate. In mid-November 1987, officials from the DIA were contacted by an Israeli businessman residing in London. This businessman stated that he had a contact in Thailand who was in a position to negotiate the release of American prisoners from Vietnam through Cambodia. In this instance, the Thai contact had provided photos of two alleged American POWs. Among the photos were several views of a disheveled Caucasian male standing amidst tall elephant grass while holding the front page of an English language Bangkok newspaper. Identification of the specific newspaper proved that the photo was taken on or after 7 November 1987. According to the Israeli businessman, the POWs could be safely and quickly released for the sum of $1.2 million.

Alerted by DIA, investigators in Thailand began to track the case, while DIA maintained communication over the following weeks with the businessman in London who steadfastly refused to name his Thai point of contact. The businessman continued to press for the money, at the same time reporting to DIA regarding alleged ongoing rescue efforts in Asia which were always depicted

Mr. Charles Strait, who posed as an American POW for individuals trying to defraud the US government.

as being on the brink of success. A confusing series of events followed, none of which were entirely clear, which included at least one supposed attempt to bring a prisoner out of Cambodia, which was allegedly turned back at the Thai border. Thereafter, though contact was maintained with the London informant, no prisoner was ever delivered.

Meanwhile, unbeknown to the man in London, the alleged POW in the photo was identified as an American who had been discharged from the US Air Force in Thailand in 1970 and had resided in a small village there with his Thai family since that time. This man, Mr. Charles Strait, freely admitted to officers at the American embassy in Bangkok that he had been recruited by a Thai friend on behalf of Thai Chinese "entrepreneurs," to pose in a photo as an American POW. It was Strait's understanding that the Chinese men had concocted the scheme to defraud some "Australians" who would supposedly pay a large sum of money for an American prisoner.

Though there were still many questions left unanswered regarding this scam, in retrospect it seems likely that the prospect of considerable reward money was the lure which drew a number of people into this particular activity. Most likely only the Chinese perpetrators had a complete grasp on the details of the fraud, while the Israeli businessman, Charles Strait, and others were only pawns (though knowingly) in the game to defraud the US government. It is ironic that, as far as can be determined, the only one who made any money on this scam was Strait, who claimed he collected $1,500 from the perpetrators of the scam for his modeling services.

It is hard not to draw a correlation between the offer of reward money and the occurrence of these various fraudulent schemes to produce an American prisoner. Seemingly, rewards have been a continuing facet of the MIA issue since shortly after the Operation Homecoming prisoner return in early 1973; indeed, as noted, the US government had used a reward program during the early days of the JCRC. Over the years, a number of individual families have advertised for information and assistance regarding lost family members. Unfortunately, an ample supply of opportunists, with the strong scent of money in their nostrils, then set out to take advantage of the misfortune of others. As a consequence, several families have been tragically cheated out of large sums of money.

Though at least one MIA activist group has had a long-standing offer of a large reward for the return of a live prisoner from southeast Asia, no group ever achieved the notoriety of a more recent offer made in the spring of 1987 by a group of eight congressmen, one former congressman, and one former prisoner of war. With much fanfare, this group announced before a gathering of press cameras that they were each pledging personal funds to a grand total of one million dollars which would be awarded to the first Asian to bring forth an American prisoner. Photos of this group, lined up behind a table piled high with stacks of money supposedly totaling the one million, were flashed worldwide and picked up for publication in newspapers, including those in Thailand.[8] In the intervening years, additional private pledges have increased this reward offer to 2.4 million dollars. More recent publicity for this fund has included such attention-getting stunts as floating notices of the reward in sealed plastic bags on the Mekong River separating Thailand and Laos, and the launching of message-carrying balloons from a boat in the South China Sea to be propelled westward by the winds into Vietnam.

The US government, for reasons earlier described, has deemed such use of rewards as a counterproductive means to bring about the release of any prisoners who may still be held. Officials maintain that rewards only complicate the resolution task and point out that thus far no POW has surfaced in spite of these well-publicized offers.

Commenting editorially on this large reward offered by the group of congressmen in early 1987, a small midwest newspaper took a different critical look at the motivation, terming it ''a safe way of playing Rambo,'' but one which raised serious questions:

A display of one million dollars in cash, representing a reward offered for the safe return of an American prisoner-of-war from Southeast Asia. Published by the *The Nation*, with credit to the Associated Press.

. . . These men, after all, are in seats of power with broad access to information. Does their reward offer mean they have some new evidence that American POWs from the Vietnam conflict are still alive and accessible to rescue?

If they have such information, they should make it known. If they don't have such evidence, it's cruel to raise new hopes among families of those who are missing in action.

Sadly, the course these men have taken argues against their reward offer being anything other than a bid for political acclaim. These congressmen not only are in a position to gain information, but they are also in a position to take action for all of us. As Republicans they have the ear of a Republican administration which carries out American foreign policy. They sit in a Congress which helps shape that policy and which can allocate money and resources far beyond a million dollars, up to the point even of declaring war.

Instead of taking any official action, they had their picture taken with a pile of money. Thus we can only assume that they either have no information on which the government can act or that they believe the government of which they are so vital a part is really powerless. Either way, they've put on a pretty sad show. Their reward money, unfortunately, is probably safe—and they undoubtedly know it.[9]

NOTES

1. Information on the early beginnings of the National League of Families is extracted from an October 1987 information sheet entitled *Background Information*, published by the League.
2. Undated letter from Skyhook II Project, Old Westbury, NY, soliciting funds to "help continue vital efforts to rescue our men from their ruthless Southeast Asian captors."

3. Undated letter (probably May 1985) from Operation Rescue, Inc., Washington DC, soliciting contributions to "keep the Akuna (an alleged refugee rescue ship) and Operation Rescue afloat."

4. Letter of 3 October 1986 from the American Defense Institute, Washington DC, soliciting funds to broadcast on national television several BBC films which "dramatically tell of evidence of live POWs."

5. DIA letter U-1520/VO-PW, dated 23 November 1987, addressed to Congressman Solarz and signed by BGen James W. Shufelt.

6. Interview of LTC (Ret) James Gritz by the JCRC Liaison Officer in the provincial jail at Nakhon Phanom, Thailand, on 2 and 3 March 1983, reported in JCRC LNO message, US-DAO BANGKOK DTG 031815Z MAR 83.

7. US House of Representatives, Hearings Before the Subcommittee on Asian and Pacific Affairs, Committee on Foreign Affairs, 22 March 1983 (98th Congress, 1st Session), p. 76.

8. See, for example, the 29 April 87 issue of the English language Bangkok newspaper, *The Nation*, which carried both a photograph of the group offering the $1,000,000 reward, plus an accompanying story headlined, "Congressmen Offer $1M Reward for Freed POWs."

9. *The Mason City* {Iowa} *Globe-Gazette*, editorial entitled, "POW Reward Offer Makes Sad Show," 30 April 1987.

5

RENEWED EFFORTS

ESTABLISHING AND MAINTAINING CONTACT

From its inception, one of the JCRC's continuing priorities was to sit down with the former adversaries and engage them in a discussion of the casualty resolution task. This was deemed a necessary prelude to the ultimate goal: to conduct an investigation into each and every case of men missing and unaccounted for.

The path to agreement for regular meetings with Vietnamese officials has never been an easy one. As previously described, the history of US/Vietnam contacts on the POW/MIA issue until the early 1980s was characterized by only occasional and sporadic meetings. In the immediate aftermath of the Paris Peace Accords, there were the non-productive Four-Party meetings in Saigon and the delayed repatriation of the remains of those Americans who had died while in captivity in the North. In succeeding years contacts were made during the aborted attempt to normalize relations, plus a few contacts on the occasion of remains repatriations, often inspired by visits to Vietnam by congressional or other US governmental delegations. Though the goal of all these exchanges was discussion of the topic of Americans still unaccounted for, only one contact during this entire period (the SRV delegation visit to the JCRC and CIL in Hawaii in July 1978) had as its focus of attention the basic "mechanics" and techniques of the casualty resolution business.

It was not until the summer of 1979, during a 3-day visit to Hanoi by a congressional delegation, that the government of the Socialist Republic of Vietnam gave indications of seriously focusing its attention on the problem of missing Americans as a continuing divisive issue which must be dealt with. At one point during discussions between delegation leader Congressman Lester Wolff (D-NY) and (then) Vice Foreign Minister Nguyen Co Thach, the latter exclaimed in English, "This is crazy! It is crazy that this issue keeps us apart for so long!"[1] During the course of these same talks and at Congressman Wolff's strong urging, Thach gave his government's "agreement in principle" to the notion of US/SRV meetings specifically held at the technical level during which casualty resolution would be the sole topic for discussion.

US officials were to learn once again, however, that there was a wide gap between "agreement in principle" and agreement implementation. In spite of US urging, the first meeting of technical personnel did not take place until over a year later.[2] This meeting, held in October 1980 in Hanoi, marked the first time that personnel from both sides, none of whom represented the policy-making level, sat down at a meeting table to discuss the "nuts and bolts" of resolving the fate of still missing American servicemen. The two US participants, both from the JCRC, were introduced to officials from the Vietnamese counterpart organization which went by the title of the "Viet-Nam Office for Seeking Missing Persons," thereafter referred to by the Americans as the VNOSMP. The membership of this VNOSMP group included a mixture of civilian and military officials from the Ministries of Foreign Affairs, National Defense, and Interior.

Though it was a step in the right direction, this first meeting fell far short of what had been hoped for. The

Americans came to the meeting prepared to lay the groundwork for a continued program of joint effort. The US participants made a special plea for the joint examination and matching of military records, explaining that the US side had only partial knowledge of what had happened to each casualty. By examining Vietnamese wartime records, they argued, the two sides had a much better chance of clarifying what had actually taken place in each loss incident.

For their part, the Vietnamese seemed more interested in explaining, in great polemical detail, why any imminent increase in cooperation was impossible. The Vietnamese spokesman, an official from the Foreign Ministry, explained their view of the United States "playing the China card" against Vietnam, and how the populace in the countryside, on whose support any further progress would depend, were well aware of the hostile United States attitude and would therefore withhold their cooperation despite the central government's sincere desire to resolve the POW/MIA issue. Consequently, little was achieved as a result of this first meeting, other than to set the precedent for later technical-level meetings which (hopefully) would be considerably more productive.

The next technical meeting, held in Hanoi nearly eight months later in May 1981, was indeed somewhat more productive. The three JCRC participants were alerted to possible progress when they learned that Vietnamese officials had granted permission for representatives from both AP and UPI wire services to travel to Hanoi, indicating a possible disclosure of "good news." At the conclusion of nearly two days of stressful talks the Vietnamese side finally made their announcement: they had been able to locate the remains of three American flyers who had perished in northern Vietnam, and would repatriate these remains in the near future.

Although Vietnamese officials provided tentative identities of the three airmen, the names were not publicly announced until later.[3] Interestingly, the remains proved to be those of three individuals from a list of four which had been previously delivered by American officials to the SRV UN Mission in New York over one year earlier. The list had been presented to the SRV delegates because these four were representative of a larger group of cases on which the United States possessed irrefutable evidence of SRV knowledge of the cases.

One of the four cases on the list was that of PFC Donald Sparks, mentioned earlier, who disappeared in the south following a skirmish with Viet Cong forces on 17 June 1969. At the time, Sparks was believed to have been killed. But in a shocking twist of fate, in May 1970, nearly a year after his disappearance, two handwritten letters authored by PFC Sparks in April 1970 were recovered by American forces from the body of a Viet Cong soldier. According to these letters to his parents in Iowa, Sparks was being held in captivity, was being reasonably well cared for, and was recovering from the wound received at the time of his capture.

In another of the four cases, the SRV had previously published (or allowed to be published) a photograph clearly depicting the identifiable body of a young aviator. The third case on the list was that of another aviator who was known to have died while in captivity. In both of these instances, the United States possessed clear evidence regarding their fate. But more importantly, it was obvious that the SRV had knowledge of their deaths, and should have known the whereabouts of their remains.

The fourth name on the list was that of Navy Lieutenant Ronald Dodge, who had become a *"cause célèbre"* among those familiar with the POW/MIA issue. Dodge had been taken into custody following the shootdown of his F–8E Crusader over northern Vietnam on 17 May 1967. He became one of the most celebrated cases when a photograph depicting Dodge accompanied by Vietnamese cadre appeared on the cover of the French magazine, *Paris Match*. Later, movie pictures were also obtained which showed Dodge wounded but alive and being escorted through a Vietnamese village following his capture. But to everyone's surprise, Lieutenant Dodge was not among the prisoners returned during Operation

Homecoming, and his name did not appear on the list provided by the Vietnamese naming those who had died while in captivity. The cry soon went up among the families, "WHAT EVER HAPPENED TO RON DODGE?", and billboards and bumper stickers featuring this question appeared nationwide.

Past US overtures regarding the Dodge case, as well as others which the Vietnamese government could obviously help to resolve, had generally been met with silence. That is, until the technical meeting on 29 May 1981, when the VNOSMP representative divulged the discovery of the remains of the three aviators, including Lieutenant Dodge, from the list of four names provided to them in New York.[4]

After the three remains were repatriated in July 1981 and the names became public knowledge, an outcry arose over the fact that Vietnam had withheld these remains for such a long period, when they supposedly could have returned them years earlier. Understandably, there was particular antagonism toward Vietnam regarding the case of Ron Dodge, who was last known to be very much alive in Vietnamese custody. The League of Families angrily termed the remains repatriation a token effort on the part of the Vietnamese government, and the US government passed a message to Hanoi demanding an explanation of exactly what had happened to Lieutenant Dodge.[5] The Vietnamese responded indignantly that it was a "hostile act" to pose such a question and, once again, progress ground to a standstill.

This incident was typical of the problems encountered in establishing and maintaining a continuing dialogue with Vietnam at the technical level. Forward progress was agonizingly slow, seemingly always with one step backward after every two steps forward. To renew contact, get the stalled technical discussions back on track, and impress upon the SRV the high priority which the US government placed on resolution of the MIA issue, a visit to Hanoi by a high level administration official was proposed. Consequently, in February 1982, Mr. Richard Armitage, then Deputy Assistant Secretary of

Defense for International Security Affairs, led a delegation to Hanoi for discussions on matters of policy. The discussions achieved only moderate success, but resulted in the SRV accepting a long-standing US invitation for a Vietnamese delegation to once again travel to Hawaii to visit both the JCRC and CIL facilities. The Hawaii visit took place approximately six months later, with the SRV delegation receiving briefings on the US approach to the casualty resolution problem.

Once again, a slight warming of the relationship followed with a corresponding increase in progress. The SRV moved to regularize the technical discussions when they agreed to hold such meetings four times per year. In October 1982 and June 1983 Hanoi repatriated the remains of additional US servicemen (four and eight respectively), and technical discussions between the JCRC and the VNOSMP took place in December 1982, March 1983, and early June 1983. Even such limited progress was not destined to last long. On 28 June 1983 Secretary of State George Shultz, while in Bangkok to attend a foreign ministers' conference of the ASEAN group of nations, commented publicly on the "cruel and heartless action" by the Vietnamese government in withholding the remains of American servicemen. The technical meetings and remains repatriations once again ground to a halt.

This pattern of "on again, off again" was to continue, with flurries of progress interrupted by periods of inaction. The Vietnamese, always sensitive to any move or action from the US side which they perceived as "hostile," were primed and cocked to withhold their cooperation at the first drop of a critical word. In some instances, the exact source of Vietnamese pique was obvious, such as when the Vietnamese sent word via the American ambassador in Bangkok that the time was "not propitious" to resume technical meetings following Secretary Shultz's remarks, or when they temporarily postponed cooperation following the 15 April 1986 retaliatory raid by the United States against Libya. At other times the reasons for cessation of activity were less obvious, such as when the Vietnamese postponed, at the very last minute, a meeting and remains repatriation scheduled for 18-21 April 1984, saying only that it was being done for "technical reasons."

During those periods when progress at the technical level came to a halt for any great length of time, the United States customarily reacted by initiating another policy-level meeting to engage high-level SRV officials in discussions. These meetings served as an essential complement to the technical discussions, often paving the way and arriving at the policy decisions needed to advance the technical activity.

In February 1984, for instance, Assistant Secretary of Defense Armitage again led a delegation to Hanoi in an attempt to increase the pace of cooperation. As a result of the discussions the Vietnamese side agreed to reopen the stalled technical talks, and to focus their investigative efforts first on the Hanoi-Haiphong area where a concentration of US losses in the north had occurred, and on attempting to recover of the remains of American servicemen who died while in captivity in the south. Later Assistant Secretary Armitage, this time accompanied by Assistant Secretary of State Paul Wolfowitz, made a third visit to Hanoi in January 1986 to meet with SRV Foreign Minister Nguyen Co Thach. The agreements were once again expanded to include a commitment from the SRV that they would conduct investigations of specific reports alleging Americans possibly still held captive. Foreign Minister Thach also pledged to attempt resolution of the POW/MIA issue within a two-year period, a commitment which the SRV later shelved.

Interspersed with these high-level discussions were a number of other meetings, some held in Hanoi, and others held at the SRV Mission to the United Nations in New York. Ordinarily the US side was represented by an official from the National Security Council, often accompanied by representatives from the Departments of State and Defense, but always accompanied by the Executive Director of the National League of Families in order to emphasize the unity of purpose between the US government and the family members of those still missing. Through these series of contacts, discussion of policy matters was emphasized while the technical experts from the JCRC and CIL concentrated on implementing the agreements reached and achieving progress on the individual cases.

TECHNICAL MEETINGS

To achieve the goal of the fullest possible accounting of missing servicemen, talk of generalities and policy matters had to come to a halt. The specifics of each individual case had to be addressed at some point. This latter task was the whole reason for the technical meetings. Typically, the US side for these meetings was composed of members of the JCRC, plus members from the Army's Central Identification Laboratory to address specifics related to the identification of remains and the techniques of proper recovery. Customarily, the JCRC Commander was the US team leader. The counterpart group from the Vietnamese side, the VNOSMP, included representatives from the SRV Foreign Ministry, the Ministry of Defense, and the Interior Ministry, with the leader being from the Foreign Ministry. A military medical doctor represented the SRV on technical questions relating to the identification of remains.

The schedules for commercial flights between Bangkok and Hanoi, resulted in the US team ordinarily traveling to Hanoi on a Wednesday, participating in meetings on Thursday and Friday, then departing Hanoi to return to Bangkok on Saturday. This schedule usually permitted ample time for presentations by both sides, plus any added special activity such as occasional trips into the countryside to view crashsites, or visits to the military museum to examine war relics which were on display. Early attempts to establish an agenda in advance or to determine if the Vietnamese hosts had any additional special activities planned generally proved futile; therefore, the US participants found it necessary to plan for any number of possible contingencies prior to each trip to Hanoi.

Planning for each meeting was extensive and detailed. Each item of discussion was cleared by the Interagency Group (IAG) in Washington, DC. Since, by definition, these meetings were to be "technical" in nature, emphasis was placed on discussion of specific loss incidents, what the United States knew of the case based on available records, gaps in US understanding of what had occurred, and specific suggestions as to how the VNOSMP might be able to assist in resolving the case. To aid the presentations by the US side, each case was prepared with a folder which contained, as a minimum, a narrative account (also translated into Vietnamese) describing the loss incident in detail, a photo and physiological information for each individual associated with the incident, a detailed map of the area of the incident or the area where the individual was last believed to be, plus any other material which might bear on the case such as clippings from Vietnamese publications or photos published by the Vietnamese during the war which were correlated to this particular case. In other words, the US side prepared and presented to the VNOSMP a package on each case which could be given to a VNOSMP investigator to enable him to go to a specific area or village, begin an investigation, and interview possible witnesses.

The subject of possible live Americans still in Vietnam was (and still is) always a topic of discussion. The JCRC spokesman became quite adept at rephrasing the question at each meeting, in an effort to foreclose on any possible loophole: "Are there any American military personnel whom you consider as criminals still being held in your jails?" "Are there any individuals from America whom you now consider as Vietnamese citizens still living anywhere in Vietnam?" The VNOSMP reply was unfailingly negative. Sometimes the reply was given resignedly with a sigh; at other times the reply was testy and exasperated. But always it was emphatically negative.

As a consequence of interviewing Vietnamese refugees throughout Asia, the JCRC had gathered and reported a number of sightings of alleged Americans in Vietnam. While many of these reports were satisfactorily resolved by the intelligence analysts, there were always a smaller number of intriguing reports which could not be clarified. During the earlier technical meetings, US suggestions that the VNOSMP assist in checking out some of these reports had gone unanswered. Following the January 1986 meeting in Hanoi between Assistant Secretary of Defense Armitage and Foreign Minister Thach, however, agreement had been reached that the SRV would cooperate in such investigations.

Subsequently, during the next technical meeting in late February 1986, the VNOSMP accepted several cases of alleged sighting of Americans for investigation. Regrettably, when investigation results were disclosed at a later meeting, the VNOSMP was able to shed very little light on any of the reports. In several instances, they reported their inability to confirm the information provided them by the US side; in one instance their investigation revealed the presence of a man who could have been reported as an American, but who proved to be of another nationality.

The idea behind the "technical meetings" was to keep them focused on case specifics, and to avoid talking of wider policy matters or topics other than the MIA issue, since these were for others at a higher level of government to discuss. Therefore, from the first meeting in 1980, the US side took great pains to make clear that the JCRC and CIL participants were not empowered to exchange views on other, unrelated topics. Such caveats, however, did not prevent the Vietnamese side from engaging in polemics or in using the US participants to deliver messages to the US government, since they knew that everything said at the meetings would be duly reported back to the Departments of Defense and State.

Consequently, whenever the Vietnamese officials wanted to make a political point, or to express their government's unhappiness over some perceived US slight or "hostile act", the VNOSMP leader would deliver the appropriate diatribe for the US side to note and forward to Washington, DC. With the passage of time, however, and as the same individuals met across the table time after time and became personally more familiar with one another, it was natural that the intensity of these polemical blasts would diminish. The VNOSMP members, who were obviously working from their own prearranged script, also began to treat these unproductive interludes to the technical talks as a matter of routine. Usually, at a certain point during the meetings the head of the VNOSMP would reach for his paper and read its typed script. He would then casually set it aside and resume the technical discussions. The Vietnamese had seemingly become as bored at making their polemical presentations as the US side was at listening to them.

FIELD WORK

While the technical meetings were an absolutely essential ingredient in the task of resolving the fate of those still missing, the real payoff would ultimately come only as a result of specific investigative activity. This activity might be excavation of graves or crashsites, visits to places of detention, interviews of villagers or witnesses, or even plowing through Vietnamese wartime government files or other sources of evidence. A part of the purpose of the technical meetings was to provide the VNOSMP with the necessary background information to begin such investigative activity, and to direct them toward what appeared, at least to the US side, the most productive path. But another important point continually made during the technical meetings was the US strong desire that Americans take part and cooperate in any investigative activity.

The desire for US on-site participation in any Vietnamese (or Lao) investigations into the fate of missing service members was not simply a frivolous desire to be involved. The very practical concerns, earlier noted, regarding the technical expertise needed to make a proper recovery of remains, plus the legal concerns relating to the "chain of evidence" and accurate documentation of the effort were paramount.

In addition, there was the factor of "credibility" to consider. It was commonly accepted, though generally unspoken, that in a great many cases an investigation—even the most honest and meticulous—would yield neither evidence that the individual under investigation was still alive, nor recoverable remains. In these instances, the best that could be offered would be a detailed report of the investigation, including statements made by witnesses, steps taken to uncover facts, places visited or searched, and so on. Given the feelings of the next-of-kin of those still missing, US officials surmised that few families would readily accept a final report rendered solely by Vietnamese or Lao authorities. Thus, American on-site presence was deemed imperative to overcome what might be bluntly termed a lack of trust in the content of a solely communist-produced report.

Early efforts to convince Vietnamese interlocutors that the United States should be included in their investigations were met with negative responses. At first reactions were to the effect that "we can do it ourselves." Later, the VNOSMP relented only to the point of occasionally permitting a visit to a site, ordinarily an aircraft crashsite, though on one occasion a visit was also arranged to a former place of detention of United States prisoners. In this way, JCRC and CIL representatives took several trips from Hanoi to the countryside to view aircraft crashsites near Haiphong, Ninh Binh, and towards Hoa Binh to the southwest. Even so, as late as August 1984 Vietnamese officials were still maintaining a rigid stance, and told visiting JCRC and CIL officers with apparent finality that they would not agree to joint conduct of investigative efforts "now or in the future."[6]

Only two months later, however, at the technical meeting held on October 1984, there were the first signs of a slight shift in the Vietnamese position regarding joint activity. The head of the VNOSMP discussed at great length the difficulties and expense involved during their unilateral search activities which had resulted in the return of remains of American servicemen. He continued to rule out joint activity, citing as the primary reason the lack of mutual diplomatic relations, but left the door open to "visits" to excavation sites by JCRC and CIL officials. This position was reiterated during the next technical meeting in February 1985, with the head of the VNOSMP making a strong bid for US assistance in the form of funds and special equipment needed to carry out SRV unilateral excavation efforts.

In early March 1985, Mr. Richard Childress of the National Security Council staff, who had either led or participated in many previous high level meetings with Vietnamese policy makers, traveled once again to Hanoi to discuss with them their cooperation on the MIA effort. At this time Vietnamese officials not only agreed to increase the tempo of technical meetings (six a year rather than four a year), but also favorably entertained the idea of carrying out joint activities with US participation. These "agreements in principle" were confirmed to JCRC and CIL personnel during the following technical meeting held in April 1985.

In mid-1985, the Vietnamese Foreign Ministry made known its desire to resolve the POW/MIA issue within a period of two years. The United States, extremely pleased with this announcement, drew up and offered for Hanoi's consideration a plan which included considerable US participation in terms of manpower, expertise, and specialized equipment support. During a policy-level meeting held in Hanoi in late August 1985, however, SRV officials ignored the US plan and instead presented their own unilateral plan of action. This plan was divided into three phases. It included an initial nationwide public information and education program for the benefit of local officials, followed by a program of collection and verification of information from throughout the country. The final phase involved excavation and recovery of any remains

135

which were discovered as a result of the second phase activity.

This Vietnamese plan was primarily unilateral in nature, envisioning that any excavation and remains recovery activity would normally be carried out by Vietnamese officials and workers. The plan did, however, allow that US help might be requested if needed. When the plan was presented, SRV officials made clear that Vietnam would not ask for any compensation, though the United States would be permitted to contribute to the cost of the activity on a voluntary basis.

Several other factors may have contributed to this gradual shift in SRV position toward allowing US participation in a joint activity. For one, Indonesia's Foreign Minister had also visited Hanoi in March, and had discussed with Vietnamese Foreign Minister Thach the need to be more cooperative and to more seriously address the American MIA issue. Perhaps even more influential, however, was the effect of a joint excavation activity at a crash site in Laos, carried out by American and Lao personnel and completed in February. There is no doubt that Vietnamese officials, after consulting with their Lao allies, learned of the potential benefit—in bilateral good will, in international public relations, and in monetary terms—which could be gained by working together with the Americans.

Regardless of the rationale, during the April 1985 technical meeting, the VNOSMP announced that they would agree to US participation in a joint excavation of an aircraft crashsite, and suggested it take place at the village of Yen Thuong, approximately 15 kilometers northeast of Hanoi, where a B–52 had crashed in December 1972. A preliminary visit to the site by JCRC and CIL officers and a review of B–52 crash records gave cause for US initial hesitation. During the preliminary look at the site, local villagers brought forward a piece of wreckage which they stated had come from the crashed aircraft. Close examination of this piece revealed the presence of Cyrillic letters stamped into the metal, indicating the likelihood of Russian manufacture, such as might be expected from a MiG aircraft or a SAM missile. During the next technical meeting in July 1985, the US side emphasized to the VNOSMP the importance to both sides of selecting a site for this first precedent-setting excavation which would provide the maximum chance of successful outcome—the recovery of identifiable remains. Though the US officials offered for consideration another site which seemed to afford a better opportunity for success, the VNOSMP officials remained adamant that the excavation would take place at the Yen Thuong site.

On 5 July 1985, JCRC, CIL, and VNOSMP officials conducted a detailed on-site survey in preparation for the eventual excavation. In this particular incident, according to local villagers the flaming aircraft had crashed into the midst of the hamlet during the nighttime, gouging a large crater in the earth, destroying a number of structures, and killing several of the local inhabitants including the husband of the old woman who currently resided at that location. Following the cessation of hostilities, the villagers had hauled away or buried any residual wreckage from the crashed aircraft, had filled in the crater formed and had then returned the area to production, in this case, a vegetable garden. Neighboring houses had been rebuilt or repaired; consequently, after the passage of over twelve years there was little visible evidence of an aircraft crash. Nevertheless, one of the important elements of this survey was to pinpoint the most logical location to begin the excavation in order to locate any possible recoverable remains of the B–52 crew.

The JCRC and CIL officers spent several hours interviewing local inhabitants, photographing and mapping the area and nearby structures, and determining the accessibility of the area from existing roads and pathways. These were all important factors to consider when deciding how many people would be needed to carry out the excavation, what particular skills would be necessary, and what specialized or unique equipment might be required.

Following several exchanges of planning data between the US and SRV groups during the ensuing months, the American team arrived at Noi Bai airport near Hanoi on 18 November 1985 aboard a USAF C–141 cargo aircraft. The excavation team, in addition to JCRC and CIL personnel, included a medic, specialists in handling and disposal of unexploded ordnance (in the event of discovery of bombs or other dangerous explosives), and military engineers to operate a large tractor-mounted digger which was also aboard the C–141 aircraft. The VNOSMP officials, in addition to coordinating the effort, arranged for the necessary guards, laborers, trucks, and other equipment needed to carry out the excavation task.

Digging began immediately, with team members commuting daily to the site from their quarters in a Hanoi hotel. As earth was excavated from the impact site, it was hauled to a nearby location for spreading and examination for possible human skeletal remains. Because of its clay-like consistency, dry screening of the soil was impossible, and clods of earth had to be carefully and laboriously broken up and examined by hand. This condition was further aggravated by rain and seeping ground water as the hole was continuously deepened. After four days without locating any remains, at Vietnamese insistence two dwellings were razed and the excavation was widened. Hopes were buoyed by the occasional discovery of aircraft wreckage such as landing gear, engine parts, fuel bladders, survival rafts, and other assorted pieces which confirmed that indeed a B–52 had impacted at this location (and not a vehicle of Russian origin as earlier thought possible). However, after over 2 weeks of digging which left a hole measuring 50 by 100 feet and nearly 40 feet deep, no identifiable remains or personal effects of the crew could be located. A few scant skeletal fragments which were initially believed to be human, later proved to be of animal origin upon detailed examination by CIL anthropologists in Hawaii.

When this excavation effort was finally terminated on 3 December 1985, there was disappointment on both sides. The VNOSMP officials and their Vietnamese workers had proven willing and helpful associates, and had done their utmost to assure that the work proceeded

American and Vietnamese workers excavate the site of a 1972 B–52 bomber crash near Hanoi in an effort to recover any identifiable remains of the crewmen.

smoothly despite the adverse weather, numerous equipment problems, and hazardous conditions.[7] In spite of the diligent work from both sides, and though the specific B–52 involved in this incident was identified with reasonable certainty, the final results were inconclusive. The JCRC Commander, LTC Joe Harvey, who led the US team's portion of the effort, rightfully surmised that it was unlikely the results would resolve the cases of the crew members aboard this aircraft.

This first joint excavation activity with the Vietnamese, though unsuccessful in terms of results, had a much wider significance in terms of precedent. Even in the absence of diplomatic relations, and despite the many previous SRV refusals, here was an instance where US and SRV officials demonstrated the ability to work together in a coordinated manner in a cooperative spirit to carry out a mutually agreed upon task. It marked one more milestone in the agonizingly slow decade-long process of instituting a reliable procedure to arrive at the fullest possible accounting of all missing personnel.

This same precedent had been set with the Lao government earlier and, as previously noted, probably had a favorable impact on the Vietnamese decision to cooperate. But in the case of the Lao as well, gaining agreement for the first excavation had been an excruciatingly slow process. Lao officials had exhibited extreme suspicion in their dealings with the United States, even though diplomatic relations existed between the two countries. Much of this was due, no doubt, to their mistaken belief that the US government was in some way supporting the ongoing noncommunist resistance effort against the Lao Peoples' Democratic Republic (LPDR).

Indeed, numerous Lao refugees in Thailand opposed the communist regime, and were actively involved in cross-border probes trying to make trouble for the Lao government. Their efforts were occasionally abetted by private US anti-communist groups and Lao refugees who had resettled to the United States. The Lao government had been particularly vocal in denouncing alleged US encouragement of the resistance activities of General

Vang Pao, the former leader of the Hmong forces in the fight against the communist Pathet Lao in the 1960s and early 1970s. After fleeing Laos in 1975, Vang Pao had resettled in the United States where he eventually acquired US citizenship, and travelled occasionally to Thailand to visit among the Hmong refugees still in the camps. Without fail, Vang Pao's visits to Thailand would prompt immediate Lao accusations of official US complicity in Lao resistance activity. Lao government officials seemed unable or unwilling to comprehend the travel freedom afforded to American citizens, or to understand the lack of official US government control over the private activities of American citizens.

In February 1983, reacting to extensive persuasive efforts by American embassy personnel in Vientiane, the Lao government finally agreed to meet with technical personnel from the JCRC and CIL to discuss casualty resolution in Laos. However, as described earlier, Lao insecurity once again immediately came to the fore as the news broke that a group led by an American citizen had crossed from Thailand into Laos in an alleged attempt to rescue American POWs. This meeting, dearly sought for the purpose of encouraging joint investigative activities, came to an abrupt and unproductive end.

Following another concerted campaign by American embassy officials in Vientiane, the Lao finally agreed to a joint US/LPDR investigative effort at the site of a C–130 crash in the southern panhandle of Laos, about 40 kilometers northeast of the town of Pakse. An American team was flown to the jungle crashsite by MI–8 helicopter in December 1983 to conduct the preliminary survey needed to plan the actual excavation of the site.

Having completed the survey and the attendant planning, the JCRC/CIL team eagerly awaited Lao approval to begin the actual excavation. But as the dry season drew to a close and rains began to threaten, inevitable delays and resistance to proceed on the part of the Lao occurred. With the onset of the monsoon rains, Lao officials insisted that further consideration had to be postponed. In February 1985, well over a year after the initial survey, the LPDR finally agreed to begin the excavation work.

From 10 to 22 February 1985, a joint team of 11 Americans and 15 Lao dug and sifted the rocky soil at the point where the C–130 aircraft had impacted almost vertically after exploding in mid-air on a dark night in December 1972. This painstaking effort yielded a sizeable quantity of highly fragmented skeletal and dental remains, plus other identifying effects from the aircraft crew. The on-site work turned out to be a model of cooperation, and the Lao government received favorable publicity for their effort as a consequence of permitting a large press group to visit the excavation site while work was still in progress. Later, Secretary of State George Shultz sent a letter to the Lao Foreign Minister thanking him for the Lao cooperation on this highly successful joint effort.

UNEVEN PROGRESS

All precedents for joint field work notwithstanding, progress in both Vietnam and Laos continued at an unsatisfactorily slow pace. US officials in Vientiane strongly encouraged the Lao government to build on the very successful joint excavation effort of early 1985, and to continue the progress throughout the year. The Lao, however, demanded some form of reciprocal US gesture before once again moving forward. Several high-level US delegations traveled to Vientiane during the year to further encourage cooperation, but little substantive progress was made. The sole exception was that the Lao government finally responded to a long-standing offer and in late summer dispatched a delegation to Hawaii for technical briefings on casualty resolution from both the JCRC and the CIL.

Finally, on 19 December 1985, after considerable controversy Congress passed a bill which deleted Laos from the list of countries prohibited from receiving US bilateral development assistance. In a "tit for tat" move, on 27 December the Lao Ministry of Foreign Affairs informed the American embassy in Vientiane of Lao approval of an early January 1986 joint survey and excavation of a second aircraft crash site, another C–130 crashsite—located in a jungled area to the southwest of Tchepone near the town of Muong Phine. A survey of this site was conducted on 3 January, and another highly successful excavation was conducted by a joint US/Lao team during the period from 17 February to 1 March 1986. But, as Lao officials once again refused to institute a continuing cooperative program of casualty resolution, another monsoon season came and went without any further progress being achieved. At year's end, the JCRC Commander issued his bleak assessment that there was "scant hope for meaningful progress when Laos allows only one excavation per year."[8]

Meanwhile, in Vietnam sustained progress was also slow in coming. Following the B–52 crashsite excavation in late 1985, SRV officials who met with Deputy Assistant Secretary of Defense Armitage in Hanoi in early 1986 had agreed to multiple joint activities in the future. Problems were encountered in implementing this agreement, however. US technical personnel had insisted that the next excavation site should have a very good chance of yielding positive results, particularly after the disappointment of the earlier effort at the B–52 crashsite. Minister Thach himself had acknowledged to Mr. Armitage a need for better cooperation between the two sides regarding future site selection. Despite these agreements and the goodwill which Vietnam could expect to accrue following a successful effort such as those already conducted in Laos, it was somewhat puzzling that the SRV continued to propose excavation sites which seemed to have little potential for success.

One such site was the alleged burial location of a pilot who supposedly died following ejection from his disabled aircraft some 120 kilometers south of Hanoi. A JCRC/CIL team taken to visit this site learned that the grave was believed to be several hundred feet out into a man-made reservoir, at a point which was under 3 or 4 feet of water. Though it would be possible to overcome the technical difficulties to exhume the pilot's remains, it became obvious during the visit that neither government

A joint American-Vietnamese team is poled across a reservoir near Thanh Hoa en route to view the site of the crash of an American aircraft.

officials nor local inhabitants were certain exactly where the burial location really was. Further, other information reported by the local inhabitants indicated that a considerable amount of investigation would be needed before a decision to dig could be made.

In spite of reservations about the sites being proposed by the VNOSMP representatives during the technical meetings, the US side had by now adopted the attitude that, to keep up the momentum of joint activity, at this point any excavation was better than no activity at all. Therefore, on the next trip by a JCRC/CIL team to Hanoi (a repatriation of US remains on 10 April 1986), the US side came prepared to leave team members and their equipment behind to participate in an excavation activity. Fortunately, by this time, the VNOSMP had given more careful thought to US reservations, and had themselves acknowledged that added research was needed before embarking on this particular effort. In addition to difficulties associated with site selection, other impediments to steady progress continued to arise. Some were significant; others were petty and resulted only in making the bilateral working environment more strained.

In mid-February 1986, a sizeable congressional delegation traveled to Hanoi to discuss a number of issues of bilateral importance, including the topic of Americans still unaccounted for. At a press conference held upon their return to the United States, several congressmen stated that Vietnamese Vice Foreign Minister Hoang Bich Son had conceded that American servicemen could still be alive at remote locations within Vietnam. On 17 February, in response to what were termed "false media reports," the Vietnamese Foreign Ministry issued a statement on this subject. In this statement, the Foreign Ministry acknowledged that Son did speak with the congressional delegation about the question of prisoners of war still alive, but pointed out that Vietnam "has many times affirmed that there has not been a single US prisoner more {sic} still detained in Vietnam. In case there are live Americans hiding themselves out of the control of the Vietnamese government, they can belong to two categories: they are either planted behind for the 'post-war plan' or they have illegally infiltrated into Vietnam since the complete liberation of South Vietnam.'' Nearly two months later, during a meeting with visiting US journalists on 13 April 1986, Vice Foreign Minister Son was again asked about statements attributed to him by the visiting US congressmen. Son was quoted as insisting there was ''no, absolutely no'' possibility that Americans were living in remote areas of Vietnam.

Regardless of what was actually said to the visiting Congressional delegation by Vice Foreign Minister Son, all members of the delegation allegedly came away from the 14-15 February 1986 visit to Hanoi firmly convinced that Son had admitted the possibility of American POWs being held in some remote area unknown to the central Vietnamese government. At the next Hanoi technical meeting which occurred less than two weeks after the congressional visit to Hanoi, JCRC and CIL representatives were treated to another diatribe about the issue of live Americans. VNOSMP officials, obviously miffed by the congressmen's version of the discussions in Hanoi, emphatically stated that their Vice Foreign Minister had said no such thing, and that the congressional visitors had apparently misinterpreted some of the discussions.[9]

Another contentious issue revolved around the SRV-proposed two-year plan for resolving the MIA issue, initially unveiled in Hanoi in August 1985. The United States had enthusiastically embraced the SRV plan, and at another policy meeting, this time at the SRV UN Mission in New York, had presented a list of actions which the United States agreed to carry out to complement and support the Vietnamese plan. The plan was further discussed in Hanoi in January 1986 during the talks, noted above, between Foreign Minister Thach and Assistant Secretary of Defense Armitage. At that time, with one joint excavation activity completed with the Vietnamese and having received a commitment of more to follow in the future, Mr. Armitage assured Minister Thach of the US willingness to support their plan to resolve the POW/MIA issue. Within several months, however, Vietnamese officials began to complain of a US "lack of commitment" to their plan. This message was first passed to the Executive Director of the League of Families in April 1986 during a meeting in New York, then later repeated by the VNOSMP to the JCRC/CIL team during a technical meeting in Hanoi in June.

In an effort to keep things on track, and head off what appeared to be an SRV reduction of effort, Mr. Childress of the National Security Council staff met in New York with the Vietnamese Deputy Foreign Minister to once again provide assurances of US support for the SRV plan. In early July, Mr. Childress delivered this same message to Foreign Minister Thach in Hanoi, along with a letter from Mr. Armitage outlining the US understanding of the agreements reached during the earlier January discussions in Hanoi. While Minister Thach took no issue with the US understanding of the previous agreements, he registered his complaint that no mention had been made of US responsibility for "creating a favorable atmosphere."[10]

Vietnamese grumbling about the US lack of commitment continued sporadically; however, within a few months the relationship between the two countries began yet another transition to a new phase. As the issue of the SRV two-year plan began to fade from importance and the SRV essentially shelved the plan, the issue of "creating a favorable atmosphere" began to take on a new, significant meaning.

NOTES

1. From the author's notes taken during the 11 August 1979 meeting between Congressman Lester Wolff and Vice Foreign Minister Nguyen Co Thach.

2. Between the time when Vietnamese officials agreed to the idea of technical-level meetings between the two sides (August 1979), and when the first meeting actually took place (October 1980), several significant events had occurred. In mid-January

1980 Congressman Wolff confronted Hanoi officials with the US belief that Vietnam had "stockpiled" an estimated 400 remains of US servicemen, a charge which Hanoi quickly and emphatically denied. Later, in June 1980 before TV cameras, Wolff chaired congressional hearings in Washington, DC, at which time the Vietnamese "mortician" publicly testified regarding Vietnam's withholding of these remains. Neither of these events was conducive to gaining prompt agreement from Vietnam to meet with US technical personnel.

3. The topic of public announcement of names associated with returned remains was of considerable concern. During earlier remains repatriations, Vietnamese authorities had made no attempt to withhold any name associations. US officials were concerned with the possibility of Vietnamese misidentifications, of which there had previously been several, and the potential emotional impact which the abrupt announcement of names would have on the next-of-kin. These factors were explained to Vietnamese officials and, to their credit, they soon agreed to withhold any public mention of individual names. Though this did not completely curtail the premature leaking of name associations to the media, invariably the leaks that did occur originated from American sources.

4. The remains of Lieutenant Ronald Dodge, Ltjg Stephen Musselman, and 1/Lt Richard Van Dyke were repatriated to US custody on 7 July 1981. Sadly, no word was forthcoming on the fate of PFC Donald Sparks, the fourth name on the list given to the SRV Mission in New York.

5. Any theories on the demise of Lieutenant Dodge are purely speculative, and a number have been proposed. He was never seen in the established prison "system" by other prisoners; thus it is likely that something untoward occurred before he could be transported from his point of capture to Hanoi. A number of scenarios have been postulated. He could have died from the shock of his wounds or the trauma of capture, for example. He may have made an unsuccessful and fatal escape attempt, or could have conceivably been wrested from his militia escorts and beaten to death by hostile villagers. As one of the realities of war, the tragic circumstances of his death may never be explained.

6. *USCINCPAC Command History, 1984* (TS), vol. II, 27 September 1985, p. 494.

7. On the second day of the excavation work, an unfortunate accident occurred when one of the American team members was struck in the head and seriously injured by the shovel of the tractor-mounted digger. Vietnamese officials admitted the man to a Hanoi hospital for emergency treatment, immediately passed word of the accident to the American embassy in Bangkok, and expedited the clearance for an American medical evacuation flight into Hanoi from Clark Air Base in the Philippines early the following morning. Vietnamese reaction to this emergency can only be termed extremely responsive and compassionate.

8. USCINCPAC message, DTG 050329Z DEC 86.

9. In an interesting sidelight to this whole interchange regarding the possibility of Americans being held captive in Vietnam, it was later learned that an American "adventurer," Mr. Robert Schwab, was being detained in a Vietnamese jail during this period. Schwab had been arrested in April 1985 by Vietnamese authorities after he deliberately sailed into Vietnamese coastal waters in an alleged attempt to rescue a former girlfriend. Schwab was eventually released on 14 August 1986 after being held captive for nearly a year and a half.

10. STATE message 211486, DTG 040956Z JUL 86.

6

TOWARD CASUALTY
RESOLUTION

"CREATING A FAVORABLE ATMOSPHERE"

Vietnam's attitude toward normalization of relations with the United States has been generally positive over the years. The SRV welcomed the idea of normalization during the period following their consolidation of the north and the south into a unified country in 1976. However, the Vietnamese invasion of Cambodia in December 1978 halted any further inclination by the United States to pursue the course of normalization. As the two countries again began their discourse on the POW/MIA issue and other bilateral matters during the early 1980s, the topic of normalization occasionally arose, but in a somewhat ambivalent manner. Vietnamese officials took the position that diplomatic exchanges should be considered as the natural state of affairs between countries. At the same time they often stated, even during the JCRC/VNOSMP technical meetings, that they were not about to beg for US diplomatic recognition, saying in effect, "We have gotten along without normalized relations with the Americans for many years; we can continue to get along without them in the future.''

Despite this stated position, there could be no doubt in the minds of those who had frequent contact with Vietnamese officials that normalization of relations with the United States was an eagerly sought goal. Private conversations revealed an element of uneasiness by Vietnamese officials over their closeness with their Soviet allies. This did not mean they had a preference for relations with the United States; it seemed more a reflection of discomfort over a degree of isolation and a lack of options in their external affairs.[1] Consequently, denials to the contrary, there seemed to be a constant desire on the part of Vietnamese officials for the United States to normalize relations with the SRV.

At technical meetings in Hanoi, VNOSMP comments were often the precursor of new Vietnamese initiatives to draw closer to the United States. Occasionally, a veritable offensive was directed at each US team member, as they were individually and informally engaged in conversation by their VNOSMP hosts on the subject of normalization of relations between the two countries. During the technical meetings of 6-9 February 1985, for example, Vietnamese team members initiated open and frequent informal conversation on US/SRV normalization of relations. During a later meeting, in July of the same year, the VNOSMP chief several times mentioned that the SRV government was very anxious to resolve quickly the MIA issue, and desired to meet with a ''high level'' US official to discuss ways to accelerate progress.

The high-level policy meetings between SRV and US officials were undoubtedly attractive to the Vietnamese government. Though it was oftentimes difficult to schedule a technical meeting between JCRC/CIL officials and the VNOSMP, it seldom was difficult to gain Vietnamese agreement to meet at a higher level. (It was seldom difficult to gain Vietnamese approval for the visit to Hanoi of US congressional delegations, either.) Indeed, during a meeting with National Security Council staff member

Richard Childress in Hanoi in July 1986, Foreign Minister Thach suggested that policy level meetings should be held between the two countries every six months.

Another subject which surfaced in discussions, and which gave rise to the possibility of drawing the two countries closer together, was the topic of a so-called American "technical presence" in Hanoi. There had been occasional speculation over the possible placement in Hanoi of a small technical group whose sole purpose would be to work with the VNOSMP on casualty resolution matters. Such a group would comprise primarily military experts from JCRC and CIL, and would in no way connote a diplomatic presence or recognition. In early June 1985, in response to the appearance of speculation in the press about the permanent stationing of a team of experts in Hanoi, the State Department prepared a response which said, *inter alia*:

> There appears at the present time to be no necessity to have our technical experts present on a continuous basis in Hanoi. Were circumstances to change, and Vietnam's cooperation to increase significantly in such a way as to require the more frequent or even continuous deployment of technical personnel, we will give it serious consideration. This would, of course, have no relation to the issue of diplomatic relations.[2]

This position was reiterated to the press when the topic arose once again in December 1985. In addition, during the Armitage/Thach discussions in Hanoi in January 1986 Minister Thach brought up the topic of a possible American presence, though both sides eventually agreed that the extent of on-going joint activity at that time did not warrant a permanent presence.[3] Another item discussed, and perhaps one of the key elements of agreement, was the position that the issue of missing Americans was indeed a strictly humanitarian matter on which progress could be made irrespective of other bilateral issues which separated the two countries, including the issue of normalization of relations.

The Socialist Republic of Vietnam (SRV) repatriated a number of American remains to US custody at Hanoi's Noi Bai Airport in April 1986.

But in spite of the Armitage/Thach agreements in Hanoi in January 1986, and the later Childress reiteration of US support (including qualified financial support) for the SRV casualty resolution plan, tangible progress once again began to wane. Technical meetings were held between the JCRC/CIL and the VNOSMP during the months of August and October 1986, and there were also two remains repatriations during the latter half of 1986. VNOSMP officials at these technical meetings increasingly mentioned the need for the US side to "have a really cooperative attitude" and to "create a favorable atmosphere so that the search for information about Americans missing in action would be fruitful."[4] At the same time, the number of remains repatriated dwindled to one on 17 September, and three on 26 November. Attempts by the United States to maintain the agreed-upon pace of six meetings per year and to schedule a technical meeting during January 1987 were rejected by the VNOSMP. A similar request for a meeting in February was also rejected. It became very obvious that once again, the level of progress was winding down.

SPECIAL PRESIDENTIAL EMISSARY

Meanwhile, during the latter half of 1986, considerable discussion took place behind the scenes in Washington DC about how to increase the tempo on the MIA issue and maintain it at a higher level. A number of ideas had been proposed, discussed, and rejected, including creation of a special presidential commission similar to that headed by Leonard Woodcock in 1977. By October 1986, President Reagan had determined to appoint a special POW/MIA emissary to Hanoi, and in February 1987 selected General John W. Vessey, Jr. for this position.

The President could not have made a wiser choice. General Vessey had retired as Chairman of the Joint Chiefs of Staff in 1985. He was intimately familiar with southeast Asia and the Vietnam conflict, having served in that theater in various positions of responsibility, including as Commander of the United States Support Activities Group (parent to the Joint Casualty Resolution Center) following the signing of the Paris Accords. But most important, General Vessey had an impeccable reputation for absolute integrity and forthrightness in dealings with others.

In mid-April 1987, US officials from Washington visited the SRV Ambassador to the United Nations to elaborate on the President's initiative, and in May further discussions were conducted in Hanoi as a prelude to a possible later visit to Hanoi by General Vessey. Vietnam's Foreign Ministry spokesman, again echoing their familiar theme, publicly warned that US/SRV relations would not improve unless General Vessey was fully empowered by the US government "to create a favorable atmosphere to a solution of the MIA problem."[5] Finally, an exchange of positive letters between National Security Advisor Carlucci and SRV Foreign Minister Thach served to confirm the Vietnamese acceptance of a trip by General Vessey to Hanoi, and established the humanitarian framework for the discussions to follow.

After stops en route for briefings at Honolulu and Bangkok, Presidential Emissary General Vessey and his party arrived at Hanoi's Noi Bai Airport aboard an Air Force special mission aircraft on 1 August 1987 for three days of talks. In addition to a staff composed of members from the National Security Council and the Departments of State and Defense, General Vessey's party included as special advisors General Robert Kingston, the first Commander of the JCRC, and Mrs. Ann Griffiths, the Executive Director of the National League of Families. Vietnamese interlocutors during the nearly three days of meetings were primarily from the Ministry of Foreign Affairs, and their delegation was led by Foreign Minister Nguyen Co Thach.

In the course of the discussions, a number of positive agreements were reached. Minister Thach committed the SRV to resuming joint efforts toward resolving the MIA issue. He agreed that their activity would initially address those most urgent cases wherein the missing individual was last known by the United States to be alive, but who did not return during Operation Homecoming. General Vessey presented some 220 such cases to Minister Thach for examination and review. Seventy of these cases were singled out for priority attention because of their particularly compelling nature, reflecting the US belief that these would be the ones most likely resolvable at some level of the Vietnamese government bureaucracy. General Vessey once again stressed to Vietnamese officials the need to also address the recovery of the remains of those whom Vietnam had previously listed as having died while in captivity in the southern regions of the country.

To facilitate Vietnamese casualty resolution activity, General Vessey reaffirmed the US commitment to assist this effort in a material sense. He specifically alluded to US willingness to conduct technical training for search teams, including visits to the JCRC and CIL in Hawaii, and to provide specialized equipment for excavation or remains recovery activity. In an effort to streamline the flow of information and to assure that both sides were working from a common information base, General Vessey also expressed a US desire to help automate the SRV's casualty data, thereby promoting compatibility between the VNOSMP and the JCRC and CIL.

In keeping with the humanitarian framework of the talks, Minister Thach brought up for discussion some of Vietnam's more urgent humanitarian problems, with a request that the United States help address these as a priority matter. General Vessey agreed that the United States would do so, within the legal constraints presently imposed on US-SRV relations, and with the further understanding that the focus of effort would first be directed toward the problems of the disabled. He and Minister Thach also agreed that cooperation would be pursued apart from any political matters dividing the two countries; and though each would assist with the other's humanitarian concerns, this work would proceed along parallel courses and not on a quid pro quo basis. To once again move the process forward, General Vessey and

Minister Thach agreed that technical talks would be resumed shortly, with one meeting of experts "to discuss next steps to resolve the POW/MIA issue, and another to discuss urgent Vietnamese humanitarian concerns."[6]

By the time they left Hanoi late on the afternoon of 3 August, General Vessey's party had participated in three plenary sessions with Foreign Minister Thach, plus four working-level meetings where the details of their agreements had been hammered out. General Vessey and Minister Thach had also met privately four times and established a mutual rapport which was to serve them well in the months ahead.

THE VESSEY-THACH AGREEMENTS

The impetus provided by the Vessey-Thach agreements set in motion a renewed series of technical meetings, two of which were immediately scheduled to address the implementation of these agreements. On 25 August 1987 two American groups flew to Hanoi, one a combined JCRC/CIL team to meet with the VNOSMP and work on the issue of casualty resolution, and the second composed of orthopedic and prosthetics experts to decide with Vietnamese public health officers and social affairs officials what could be done to provide relief for the many disabled amputees throughout Vietnam.

In keeping with the course agreed upon between General Vessey and Minister Thach, the JCRC/CIL team concentrated on presentation of additional details relating to the 70 "compelling cases" to receive initial priority. The VNOSMP, for their part, reported on the results of their on-going unilateral efforts to track down leads in the countryside, and to locate the remains of missing Americans. Meanwhile, in another nearby meeting room, the prosthetics experts were discussing with Vietnamese officials the extent and nature of the problems of amputees and others with crippled limbs throughout Vietnam, and preparing for a field trip to a facility for the manufacture of prosthetic devices.

Both sides felt the pressure to achieve positive results. The Vessey-Thach discussions had generated high expectations, and both the POW/MIA group and the prosthetics group were keenly aware of the need to achieve visible and substantive progress without delay. Nearly a decade and a half had elapsed since the cessation of hostilities between the two sides, yet there had been such relatively meager progress—no definitive answer to the possibility of Americans still held captive, and fewer than 150 remains of missing Americans returned from Vietnam.

For their part, Vietnamese officials surely felt that added cooperation would improve the atmosphere between their country and the United States, and would move them closer to normalized relations. Indeed, the US position, enunciated many times to Vietnamese officials, included the caveat that while resolution of the MIA issue was not a precondition for normalization of relations, the pace of normalization would be affected by the perception of the American people regarding Vietnamese cooperation on this issue.

Thus began a double series of technical discussions in Hanoi following the initial meetings by both the POW/MIA groups and the prosthetics groups. In November 1987 the prosthetics experts returned to Hanoi to discuss the report which they had published as a result of their earlier fact-finding visit in August.[7] This report, which detailed the extent of the amputee and crippled limb problem faced by Vietnam, suggested a number of remedial actions which US non-governmental organizations (NGO's) might take to help Vietnam to alleviate the situation. The US State Department rallied a number of these organizations with potential interest in assisting Vietnam to address this humanitarian problem, In December Vietnam hosted a representative group of these NGO's who traveled to Hanoi for a firsthand look at what projects might be undertaken.

By early 1988, NGO efforts were underway to procure and ship to Vietnam a number of commodities needed in the manufacture of prosthetic devices. By mid-year, some $100,000 worth of supplies had already been sent, and another 39,000 pounds of additional supplies were en route to Vietnam by ship.[8] In addition, an exchange of letters between Minister Thach and General Vessey in May 1988 led to further agreement to broaden the on-going humanitarian cooperation to include the problem of child disabilities. This agreement was immediately followed by a visit to Hanoi in early June by a four-man US medical team to explore steps to be taken.

Meanwhile, on the POW/MIA side of the Vessey/ Thach agenda, the renewed technical discussions were also beginning to show positive results. The VNOSMP, in a more forthcoming manner and in more detail than ever before, began reporting the results of their unilateral activities. Their field teams were spending more and more time in the countryside investigating possible leads and talking to villagers. The repatriation of American remains began anew, with three remains turned over to a US team in Hanoi on 27 September 1987, and another five remains repatriated on 25 November.

A new level of openness was achieved as the effort moved into 1988. Technical meetings were characterized by more give-and-take as specific information was exchanged, and discussions became more frank and detailed. The VNOSMP presented the results of their own investigative efforts, including additional reports which they alleged had come from the populace. However, a continuing source of difficulty was the "remains trading" which was taking place. The VNOSMP had obtained many such remains from the populace, particularly from the southern parts of Vietnam, and had subsequently included a sizeable number of these remains, usually later proven not to be those of Americans, among the 17 remains repatriated on 2 March, the 27 repatriated on 6 April, and the 25 repatriated on 13 July 1988.

In addition, a list of equipment to be turned over for specific use by the VNOSMP to enhance the efficiency of their casualty resolution efforts was drawn up. As the equipment items were procured, another visit to Hawaii by a VNOSMP delegation was planned. One of the primary reasons for this visit, which occurred in late June

1988, was to provide the opportunity for special training for Vietnamese operators on some of the equipment to be turned over. Such training was considered essential, particularly on such technical equipment as the computer, and to a lesser degree with the photographic gear, metal detectors, and other specialized laboratory equipment.

On 8 June 1988, General Vessey traveled to New York to meet again with Foreign Minister Thach who was there to attend a meeting of the United Nations General Assembly. This meeting provided the opportunity for mutual review of progress since their initial meeting in Hanoi ten months earlier. While the review led to a reemphasis of the importance of resolving the so-called ''compelling'' cases, there was an even more significant outcome to this meeting. During their discussions, Minister Thach revealed to General Vessey that the Vietnamese government was preparing for additional joint activity, and that they were ready to discuss the conduct of joint investigations and the possible joint excavation of suitable crashsites.

As in the past, the road to this new plateau of progress and commitment was not an entirely smooth one. Minister Thach had, on a number of occasions since their first meeting, communicated with General Vessey regarding a variety of topics not related to the humanitarian issues which had dominated their face-to-face talks. For example, in December 1987 Minister Thach had written to General Vessey to express his government's displeasure over a potential submission to the US Congress of a bill which would permit the United States to satisfy private American claims against Vietnam by liquidating Vietnamese-owned assets in the United States. In April 1988, Minister Thach wrote again, responding to a statement by a DOD spokesman who had said that Vietnam had more information about missing Americans than they had thus far divulged. On 31 July 1988, Minister Thach again wrote to General Vessey, this time expressing his views regarding a statement made by an Assistant

Secretary of State indicating that the United States should continue its policy of diplomatically isolating Vietnam.

In each of these instances, Minister Thach included the suggestion, either implicitly or explicitly stated, that the offensive US behavior jeopardized future Vietnamese cooperation on resolution of the US humanitarian problems. Fortunately, however, and indicative of the mutual rapport and respect which arose between these two men, the messages between General Vessey and Minister Thach were invariably polite, moderate in tone, and always couched in non-inflammatory terms. The various opposing positions did not become so hardened as to defy resolution, and could be reviewed unemotionally as the obstacles were removed one at a time in an effort to continue toward resolving both countries' humanitarian concerns.

Nowhere was this more evident than in the instance cited earlier where Vietnam had taken offense regarding the comments of an Assistant Secretary of State. These comments had been made in open testimony before a subcommittee of the House Foreign Affairs Committee which was holding hearings on a proposed bill calling for the President to normalize diplomatic relations with the Socialist Republic of Vietnam. When, on 31 July, Minister Thach wrote specifically that cooperation with the United States would be "temporarily suspended" as a consequence of the negative testimony of the Assistant Secretary of State, the sponsors of the normalizing bill immediately withdrew their support and all further consideration of the proposed legislation ceased. In earlier years, such a confrontation undoubtedly would have led to an extended cessation of all cooperation. Throughout this episode, however, the tenor of the communication between Minister Thach and General Vessey was kept low-key, the result being that cooperation soon afterward was not only resumed, but resumed at a level not previously achieved.

The specifics of this new level of cooperation were worked out at the next technical meetings held in Hanoi in mid-September 1988 between the VNOSMP and

JCRC/CIL officials. The plan called for the initial fielding of two joint teams, composed of both US and Vietnamese members. Each of these teams would attempt to locate and investigate several casualty-related sites during a period of approximately 10 days.

The US team members arrived at Hanoi's Noi Bai airport aboard a USAF C–141 on 25 September 1988. Also aboard the aircraft were four Jeep Cherokee 4-wheel drive vehicles to serve the transportation needs of the investigation teams, plus another 13,000 pounds of specialized equipment earlier agreed upon. After some additional logistical planning and joint consultation in Hanoi, the respective Vietnamese and American members divided into two investigation teams and departed for several specific preplanned areas in the Vietnamese countryside. On each joint team, the US contingent included a Vietnamese-speaking chief and an analyst familiar with the casualty cases under investigation, both from the JCRC, plus a CIL representative knowledgeable in the techniques of search and recovery of remains. The following week was spent travelling about, investigating leads earlier gathered by the VNOSMP, and conducting detailed interviews with local inhabitants and officials who might be able to shed additional light on the fate of those crewmen associated with the crashsites under investigation. In this way, by the time the American team members departed Vietnam on 5 October to finalize the reports of their findings, the two teams had investigated, in extensive detail, a total of six sites.

The complexity of this effort cannot be overstated. The conditions under which such work must be carried out are difficult to comprehend unless one has spent considerable time travelling about remote areas of Southeast Asia. What appear on maps as major highways are often unpaved and narrow trails, made even more difficult by the adverse weather conditions. Crashsites, when they can be located at all, are often accessible only by foot through difficult terrain and dense vegetation. Investigation team members also contend with some of the same hardships and dangers as those encountered by American infantrymen over two decades ago—from jungle leeches to unexploded anti-personnel bomblets.

The effects of time and local inhabitants' scavenging of metal debris, added to the initial effects of impact and fire, make location and identification of specific aircraft crashsites extremely difficult. One must understand that specific aircraft identification is important for several reasons. Identification of the aircraft provides the initial clues as to the possible identity of any remains which might be located at the crashsite. In addition, the Indochinese countryside is cluttered with the wreckage of several hundreds of aircraft which are of no interest from the standpoint of casualty resolution. These are the sites from which the aircrew members were known to have escaped from their aircraft prior to the crash. There is no reason to expend the effort to excavate such sites in a fruitless endeavor to locate remains which are not there. American investigators were also to encounter other difficulties in addition to those of a physical nature. Problems resulted from the multi-layered bureaucratic system which historically exists throughout the country.

The Vietnamese contingent on the joint teams normally included a representative from the Foreign Ministry, the Ministry of Defense, and the Ministry of Interior. After leaving Hanoi and arriving at the province in which the investigation site is located, comparable provincial officials had to be contacted for purposes of coordination. Team members are invariably obliged to call upon officials of the province foreign office, the province military office, and the province security office. This procedure is then repeated at the district level, and at the village and hamlet level where the people's committees hold forth in any dealings with the local populace. As a consequence, a considerable amount of time can be spent satisfying the bureaucratic requirements, explaining at each level what is planned and for what purpose, gaining agreement for any needed support such as guides and workers, or canvassing for possible eyewitnesses to interview. To comprehend the need for this time-consuming process, one needs to recall that communication systems, such as the sophisticated telephone or radio networks common in many other countries, do not exist in many of the remote areas where these investigation activities take place.

Another significant difficulty encountered relates to the interviewing of witnesses. Because of the elapsed time and wartime movement of the population, it is sometimes difficult to find people with firsthand knowledge of the event under investigation. Even if witnesses can be found, memories are often dimmed by time, and it is not unusual to obtain conflicting reports from several individuals, all of whom claim to be reporting the same event.

The question of candor on the part of witnesses has been raised when evaluating the results to date. No doubt there have been instances where the alleged witness has been coached to modify his testimony regarding the events which took place. However, with the passage of time and the increase of familiarity and trust among members of the joint teams, US investigators have reported increasing success in selecting people at random to talk to, with a corresponding increase in apparent validity of the information collected.

As noted earlier, during the first ten-day joint effort in September and early-October 1988, the two teams were able to investigate six aircraft crashsites located to the north and northwest of Hanoi. This effort was shortly followed by a second iteration beginning in late October, again with two joint teams. This time another eight cases were investigated, all to the west and southwest of Hanoi. Meanwhile, another exchange of letters took place between General Vessey and Foreign Minister Thach wherein both expressed their mutual satisfaction with the direction that the joint effort was taking, and with the results to date. Both men also agreed to further expand the on-going efforts with the fielding of additional teams.

As a result, a third joint investigative activity took place from 5 to 15 December 1988, this time in the narrow central regions of Vietnam in the area southward from Vinh toward the city of Hué. For this particular effort, three investigative teams were fielded, and they conducted investigations of 12 separate sites. In addition, a special team composed of forensic anthropologists from the CIL plus Vietnamese counterparts were in Hanoi examining, screening, and analyzing skeletal remains which had been recovered earlier from various locations throughout Vietnam. This was a special effort to address the problem, noted earlier, of copious remains obtained from "remains traders". Most of such remains had proven not to be those of American servicemen.

As the joint investigation activity picked up momentum, so also did the repatriation of remains believed to be those of Americans. On 1 November 1988, the SRV turned over 23 containers of remains, and on 15 December another 38 were repatriated. Some of these remains resulted from the efforts of the joint teams; others were obtained unilaterally by the SRV government from the populace or as a result of their own recovery activity. Among these remains were those previously reviewed by the joint forensic team and deemed to require additional scientific analysis back at the CIL in Hawaii to conclusively determine if they were those of American servicemen.

PARALLEL PROGRESS IN LAOS

The year of 1988 also saw an increase in cooperation with the Lao government on the MIA issue. Relatively little progress had been made on the casualty resolution issue in Laos since the successful excavation of the C–130 crashsite near Muong Phine in early 1986. Lao officials, in their contacts with American embassy personnel, had continued to insist on reciprocal humanitarian gestures by the United States before they would cooperate any further. During August 1987 another US policy level delegation traveled to Vientiane and elicited Lao agreement to resume cooperation. The United States agreed to work with Lao officials to resolve their humanitarian problems within the various constraints imposed by Congress. Despite these agreements, when a round of "consultative meetings" (which included representatives from the JCRC and CIL) was convened in Vientiane on 10-14 November 1987, the Lao representatives backed away from their earlier commitments to take specific actions relating to the resolution of American casualties in Laos, and once again sought specific US assistance as a precondition to any further cooperation.

The year 1988, however, began with the Lao government in a more conciliatory mood. In January, Vientiane officials agreed to receive the Commander of the CIL to discuss a number of technical concerns related to the recovery and identification of remains. On 17 February, Laos repatriated to US custody two containers of remains which resulted from Lao unilateral recovery efforts at two crashsites in the southern provinces of Saravane and Savannakhet, the first such unilateral Lao action in nearly a decade.

In addition, after a hiatus of over two years, the Lao government agreed to a survey of an aircraft crashsite, located in the old "Ho Chi Minh trail" area northwest of the town of Tchepone, followed in early May by a week-long joint excavation effort. This site was conclusively determined to be that of an Army OV–1A Mohawk aircraft, lost on 15 March 1966. Though only sparse personal effects were located, and no identifiable remains, the cooperation among the Lao and American team members, as on previous occasions, was again outstanding.

Very significant to future casualty resolution efforts, however, was the outcome of a second round of "consultative talks" held in Vientiane on 22-23 August 1988. Lao officials agreed, for the first time, to give serious consideration to a year-around program of activity, breaking away from the previous mode of permitting field work only during the relatively few dry months in the early part of each year. This was a concession the US side had long considered as vitally necessary if meaningful results were ever to be achieved on the MIA issue in Laos. In her report on the results of this meeting, the American Chargé d'Affaires, Harriet Isom, characterized the talks as the "most cordial, easy, open, and productive" sessions that US participants could recall with the Lao.[9] Only two months later, Lao officials made good on their commitment to improve cooperation. In September a JCRC/CIL team spent several days conducting preliminary surveys of aircraft crashsites in eastern Savannakhet province in preparation for future excavation activity.

In late October Laos once again sent a team of officials to Hawaii for DOD-hosted consultations with JCRC and CIL personnel, the first such visit in more than three years. In December another joint excavation effort took place at one of the crash sites surveyed in September. This site, located in eastern Laos near the Vietnam border, was that of a RF–8G Navy fighter-reconnaissance aircraft which had been lost on 28 March 1968. The joint teams were successful in recovering identifiable remains of the sole crewman.

1988, TURNING THE CORNER

The year closed as one of the most productive yet from the standpoint of cooperative efforts with both Laos and Vietnam. Unquestionably, the willingness of the United States to assist these countries in addressing their own humanitarian problems had a great deal to do with this cooperation. In Laos, for example, the United States had facilitated the shipment of a prefabricated medical clinic donated by the humanitarian non-governmental organization, Americares. All materials for the construction of this clinic, for a village in southern Laos, were transported to Laos in September 1988, and the construction work was completed by early November. Also indicative of improving US-Lao relations was the announcement, in December, that the United States and Laos would undertake expanded bilateral discussions early in 1989 in Vientiane. Significantly, the Lao expressed their willingness to include in these discussions, for the first time since

1975, the subject of narcotics control. This particular topic had prompted mutual animosity and was the source of many of the legislative restrictions that limited the US ability to assist in other Lao humanitarian concerns.

Lao cooperation may also have benefited from and been stimulated by the improved atmosphere which characterized the casualty resolution effort with Vietnam, particularly the Vessey initiatives. US humanitarian assistance in Vietnam had gone forward, and the earlier prosthetics effort was expanded to include the problems of disabled children. In July 1988 the State Department had published the results of the investigative visit to Hanoi conducted by a small group of medical specialists in early June.[10] American and Vietnamese officials continued to meet, both in Hanoi and New York, to refine and expand on ways of dealing with Vietnam's humanitarian problems. Materially, Vietnam was assisted by the shipment, in November, of substantial donations of pharmaceutical supplies to help in some of the problems of child survival. Additionally, in response to other problems set forth in the State Department report, a private group, Operation Smile, visited Vietnam in August to set the stage for a later visit by volunteer surgeons who would conduct numerous operations to repair cleft lips and palates, and other disfiguring disorders among children.

Compared with previous years, the tally of activity indicated that 1988 had been a most successful year in matters of casualty resolution. A total of six technical meetings had been held in Hanoi between the JCRC/CILHI and their VNOSMP counterparts, with the exchange of information becoming more detailed and frank. Two similar meetings had been held with Lao officials in Vientiane. American teams had participated, for the first time ever, in joint in-country investigation activity in Vietnam, with a fair amount of progress made toward addressing the 70 "compelling" cases stressed by General Vessey and Minister Thach. The SRV had unilaterally provided information—but no remains—on 11 of these 70 cases, had repatriated the remains associated with another 14, and US-SRV teams had jointly conducted field investigations on another 18 with the results yet pending.[11] Teams surveyed a number of crashsites in Laos, and two were excavated. Both Laos and Vietnam had sent delegations to Hawaii during the year for special orientation and familiarization on casualty resolution procedures. Three remains had been repatriated from Laos, and 130 from Vietnam; the CIL had been able to make positive identifications on the remains of 26 American servicemen and return these remains to their next-of-kin, while additional identification work continued on other repatriated remains.[12]

After so many years of halting progress, finally it seemed there was cause for optimism regarding the direction being taken toward resolving the fate of those still missing and unaccounted for. No one familiar with this effort would be so bold as to predict smooth sailing for all future endeavors; however, new levels of cooperation had definitely been achieved, and new precedents had been set. Nearly sixteen years of governmental attention and diligent work had finally brought the effort to this point where one might optimistically suggest that the rudimentary procedures for eventual resolution of the cases were in place. Seemingly, from the field standpoint, the task now being faced was to focus on speeding and expanding the effort, and making the activity more efficient. For those in Washington, DC, the challenge was to provide the necessary personnel and material assets to maintain and build on the momentum already attained. Anticipating and heading off potential policy problems likely to hinder the overall cooperation was another important activity.

MORE RECENT PROGRESS IN VIETNAM

The year of 1988 was clearly a year of change, not only in the tempo of casualty resolution activity, but also in the attitude of the Indochinese states. It seemed they had at last begrudgingly acknowledged that the MIA issue was indeed important to the American people, an issue which wasn't going to disappear with time. There appeared to be a realization that the casualty resolution problem must be addressed once and for all if favorable relations were ever to be restored between the Indochinese countries and the United States, their former adversary.

A review of more recent activity bears out the observation that a conscious decision has now been made to remove the issue of Americans unaccounted for in Southeast Asia as a divisive obstacle to better relations. If the amount of activity can be used as a measure of progress, a great deal has been accomplished in the past three years. Furthermore, as activity has increased, the immense difficulties of the task have become more and more obvious to all concerned.

In Vietnam, American and Vietnamese personnel have been blended together into joint teams which travel the back roads of the countryside in flashy Jeep vehicles attracting curious crowds as they investigate cases, interview villagers, and follow leads. Such activity, not long ago believed to be almost impossible, has now become so commonplace that it is seldom noted by the newspapers. Physical anthropologists from the Army CIL have routinely joined with medical counterparts in Hanoi and Ho Chi Minh City to pore over quantities of skeletal remains, measuring, comparing, and deliberating on their origin and identity. This investigative effort has led, in turn, to the repatriation of additional remains to the CIL for final identification and eventual return to their next-of-kin.

The complexity of remains recovery and identification after such a prolonged period of time, underscored by the recent investigations, have, at the same time, suggested the likelihood of non-recovery of many remains. There have been instances of bodies buried in unmarked jungle graves or fallow rice paddies, with their exact location lost from memory, even from the memories of those who were personally involved in the original interment of the remains. In other cases, the ravages of time, natural elements, erosion, and predators have made the recovery of identifiable remains highly unlikely.

At the policy level, Presidential Emissary General John Vessey made a second trip to Hanoi, meeting with Foreign Minister Thach in late October 1989. Commitments to speed the casualty resolution work were reaffirmed and expanded. So also were commitments for the United States to assist in addressing Vietnam's humanitarian concerns. US non-governmental assistance was expanded, and the government has expedited the transfer to Vietnam of medical equipment which is serviceable but no longer needed or used by US Government hospitals.

Meanwhile, moves have also been made to further ease tensions between the United States and Vietnam. The SRV set the stage when they finally withdrew their troops from Cambodia in the latter part of 1989, a move urged by the United States for many years. On 18 July 1990 Secretary of State James Baker publicly announced the US withdrawal of recognition from the Khmer Rouge faction, and signalled a possible accommodation with Vietnam when he added that talks would soon begin with the SRV. On 6 August 1990, US and Vietnamese officials met at the United Nations offices in New York to discuss a settlement of the Cambodian conflict, the role of the UN in this effort, and the need for international guarantees of neutrality for Cambodia.

Finally, on 29 September 1990, Secretary Baker and SRV Foreign Minister Nguyen Co Thach met in New York. A *Washington Post* article the following day termed this "the first high-level meeting between officials of their two countries since 1973, two years before the end of the Vietnam War." Minister Thach later hinted in a press interview that he and Secretary Baker had discussed a schedule for the establishment of diplomatic relations between the two countries. It wasn't until 9 April 1991, however, that US and SRV officials met once again to discuss the steps to be taken which would lead to normalized relations. These steps, referred to in the media as a "road map," would begin with mutual agreement on a solution to the Cambodian problem, and would end at some future date with the establishment of full diplomatic relations between the United States and the Socialist Republic of Vietnam. At intermediate points along this "road," both sides would take certain specified actions; for example, the United States would lift restrictions previously imposed on American business and veterans groups wanting to travel to Vietnam. During later steps the US trade embargo would be lifted and US opposition to international lending to Vietnam would be halted. Vietnam, in turn, was expected, among other things, to speed their work on accounting for missing US personnel.

Significantly, General Vessey made yet another trip to Hanoi later the same month. His discussions with Minister Thach resulted in a landmark agreement that a temporary office would be opened in Hanoi, manned by US casualty resolution personnel, and intended to improve the coordination between US and SRV casualty resolution personnel, as well as speed the on-going joint field investigation efforts. The establishment of this office— a suggestion discussed on and off for years but never implemented—represented a large step forward in the overall progression of relations between the United States and Vietnam. Not since the closing of the US Consulate in Hanoi in the mid-1950s had US officials been based for any extended length of time in northern Vietnam. Opened in May, the office was first manned by two officials, one from the JCRC and one from the Defense Intelligence Agency, though additional personnel were added later.

The JCRC official, because of the increased tempo of activity by visiting US investigative teams, was responsible for liaison with the VNOSMP, and for the preplanning and logistical support which were so vital to the success of the joint team activities. The primary task of the DIA member was to research with various SRV offices records and archival materials which might shed added light on the fate and disposition of Americans still missing. Such an effort, urgently sought from the time of the first US/SRV meeting in 1980, was needed to fill the voids in the incomplete US knowledge of the missing.

The United States was anxious to discover the precise fate of many whose circumstances of loss were still unknown, and to provide corroboration of any information that had surfaced during the on-going field investigation activity.

Extensive DIA research of wartime intelligence reports had led to the conviction that such archival records existed within several Vietnamese organizations. Foreign Minister Thach, interviewed while in New York in October 1990, implicitly acknowledged that such documents had been created, but at the same time hinted at the problems of locating these records.[13] "I try my best," he was quoted as saying, "but some of the archives have been bombed by the United States." In addition, records had deteriorated because "we are a tropical country and have no air conditioning," Thach continued. "It is amazing that you think other (countries) will be just like the United States" (regarding preservation of historical records), "but it is not the same."

Nevertheless, with a limited degree of cooperation from Vietnamese officials, the DIA member of the Hanoi office has been able to gain access to a number of very useful documents, including records of wartime artifacts stored or on display at the Hanoi military museum. Among the items displayed are various identity cards—such as military ID cards and Geneva Convention cards—pilots' helmets and other flight gear (many with names still affixed), weapons and aircraft wreckage (with traceable serial numbers), and other assorted detritus of war. The real value, however, is not in these items themselves, but in the documentation which accompanies them or which describes their origin. Generally, each displayed item has on file an accession document which describes the provenance of the item, and the circumstances leading to its acquisition by the museum.

While museum documentation has added to our knowledge of the circumstances of disappearance of a number of servicemen, other archival collections hold promise of even more useful information. Consequently, the DIA member of the Hanoi office has devoted considerable effort toward gaining access to the archives of various military units such as anti-aircraft units, the PAVN units which had jurisdiction over the Ho Chi Minh trail areas, and the headquarters of the forces which operated in the southern part of Vietnam. This task has produced mixed results. Varying degrees of access to military archives have been granted, but some Vietnamese officials have yet to overcome their penchant for secrecy, even when they must know their national interests are better served by openness with American officials.

The archival and records research activity in Hanoi is but one indication of DIA's expanded operational role in recent years. During the latter part of the Reagan administration, more and more emphasis was placed on acquisition of casualty resolution information, particularly as it applied to the investigation of reports of sightings of alleged live American POWs. In 1987 DIA made the decision to supplement the efforts of the JCRC personnel located in Bangkok, and assigned a small group of language qualified personnel to the task of gathering any information which might relate to possible live Americans still in Indochina. This new DIA group, code-named Stony Beach, immediately began to conduct interviews of refugees and other potential information sources throughout Asia. More recently, as joint investigative activities in Vietnam and Laos have placed increasing demands on the small JCRC liaison office staff, the Stony Beach group has assumed an even greater portion of the information gathering workload.

MOVEMENT IN LAOS AND CAMBODIA

Vietnam has not held the monopoly on increased casualty resolution activity during the past several years. Progress has also been made in Laos. The start of the rainy season no longer signals the absolute cutoff for any

possible field activity. Parties of American and Lao officials, flying aboard Russian-built Lao Air Force helicopters, have jointly visited and surveyed a number of
aircraft crashsites located among the remote mountainous
outcroppings and jungle valleys. A number of these sites
have now been successfully excavated with the resultant
recovery of identifiable remains of the crews. Additional
investigation and excavation activity is continuing.

Bilateral cooperation in addressing the humanitarian
concerns of Laos have paralleled the increase in Lao cooperation on resolution of the MIA issue. US funds and
military expertise have been used since early 1991 to
carry out a number of construction projects in more remote areas. Army engineers were responsible for the construction of a badly needed school in Savannakhet
Province which was formally turned over to the Lao government in March 1991. Additional construction projects
have been undertaken since that time. US medics or doc-
tors, always included as members of joint investigation
or excavation teams, have routinely donated their time
to provide medical assistance to rural Laotians and villagers in the vicinity of the team's casualty resolution activities. At the national level, official US aid to Laos has
assisted with Lao developmental needs, including education, health care, crop substitution and, narcotic suppres-
sion programs.

Even in Cambodia, with its slightly over eighty
Americans yet unaccounted for, there is now evidence of
a quickening activity on the MIA issue. Previously, because the US did not want to lend legitimacy to the Phnom Penh government, contact was minimal and carried
out through intermediaries. Though the communications
problem may have hampered progress, there were serious
questions as to whether Phnom Penh officials could assist
in the casualty resolution effort, even if they were inclined
to do so.

Finally, a thaw in relations began when Phnom Penh
announced a willingness to repatriate a group of remains
which they believed to be those of American servicemen.

A JCRC/CILHI delegation was dispatched to Cambodia, and on 26 July 1990 at Phnom Penh the US delegation took custody of six remains and flew them to the CILHI for further analysis.[14] When—also in July 1990—Secretary of State Baker announced a switch in US policy toward Cambodia, the stage was set for a further warming of relations between the United States and the Phnom Penh faction that was competing with other groups to control Cambodia. By the closing months of 1991, with the 23 October signing in Paris of a UN-sponsored peace agreement, the United States finally reestablished a diplomatic presence to Cambodia. The arrival in Phnom Penh of Ambassador Charles Twining brought an end to the period of non-recognition that began when Ambassador John Gunther Dean lowered the American flag there nearly 17 years earlier.

LOOKING BACK

It is sad that it has taken so long to arrive at the point where one might prudently believe that a glimmer of light can be seen at the end of the tunnel. Only now, after nearly two decades, is the US Government at the point it had earlier hoped to reach during the tenure of the Four Party Joint Military Commission in early 1973. One cannot help but wonder, "Could we have done better?"

In retrospect, it seems inevitable that the resolution of the POW/MIA issue would be held hostage to whatever concessions the Indochinese states could wrest from the United States. In simple terms, they have something which the United States wants, and it has been a seller's market. They own the territory on which most investigations would have to take place, they control the individuals who might be able to shed light on the fate of missing American servicemen, and the military and government records which might reveal what happened to our missing comrades are also in their sole charge. To paraphrase the words of an often-seen bumper sticker, "Only Hanoi can help us find out!"

The task of gaining Vietnam's cooperation (as well as that of Laos and Cambodia) has been hampered in a number of ways. Progress has been slowed by the fact that, for better or worse, the MIA issue has become intertwined with a number of other bilateral concerns. These include the problems of refugees, re-education camp detainees, and Amerasian children; the tragic and confused situation in Cambodia; the degree of cooperation on narcotics interdiction and control—and a host of other bilateral or international issues. One small example of this intertwining from earlier years was the obvious connection between Hanoi's repatriation of American remains and US actions regarding Vietnam's application for membership to the United Nations. Even in today's relatively less adversarial relationship between the United States and Vietnam, efforts to treat the MIA topic as a humanitarian issue "separate from other political problems which divide our countries" are obscured by other issues.

Another factor which has slowed progress is the extremely limited US ability to influence Vietnam. The United States, since 1973, has foregone the use of any "stick", leaving only the "carrot" as an enticement to action. This "carrot" has been commonly understood to mean a closer and more benevolent relationship with the United States, with all the attendant benefits this implies. One might conclude that the poor record during earlier years indicates that perhaps either the carrot wasn't tempting enough, or that Vietnam was not yet that hungry.

The idea that the United States should postpone any progress on the MIA issue while awaiting a change of heart by the Vietnamese has held a certain appeal for some people. For example, during a private conversation at a cocktail party in Bangkok some years ago, a Thai diplomat who had closely followed American attempts to deal with Vietnam on the POW/MIA issue drew an interesting analogy. "The American government," he said, ''is like a man in the market, unaccustomed to the techniques of bargaining, trying to buy a vase which has caught his eye. The man tells the merchant, 'I really like that vase! The color is absolutely perfect, and it has the most unusual shape. It would fit beautifully in our living-room, my wife would love it, and I must have it. Now, how much do you want for it?' ''

The implications of this analogy notwithstanding, adopting a policy of ''benign neglect'' in our dealings with Vietnam on the POW/MIA issue has never been considered a viable alternative. Not only does it run contrary to Americans' impatience to achieve results as quickly as possible, such a course of action would never have been tolerated by the family members. Even more to the point, such a ploy likely would have achieved little anyway.

Another factor in the limited amount of progress achieved, perhaps the dominant one, has been the barrier of mutual distrust existing between the United States and Vietnam. The Paris Accords left no clear victors or losers, and led not to reconciliation, but to continuing suspicion and prolonged adversarial relations. The relentless continuation of military pressure by DRV and PRG forces that resulted in the eventual collapse of the Saigon government left a legacy of bitterness over the outcome of the conflict. Some elements of the American public—and some American officials—still show signs of wanting to fight the war anew. As regards the MIA issue specifically, numerous instances of obvious SRV deception and lack of candor have strengthened American distrust of the ''humanitarian spirit'' touted by the Vietnamese.

Though occasions of duplicity and deception still occur in Vietnam's dealings on the MIA issue, happily, in recent years Vietnamese officials have exhibited a marked increase in candor—possibly perhaps their own form of *glasnost*—which has contributed to a reduction of hostility toward Vietnam. A vivid example of this change was Hanoi's response to an unusual incident that occurred in July 1988. A US Navy T–39 jet executive aircraft suffered navigation equipment failure while on a flight over the South China Sea, became lost, ran out of fuel, and was forced to ditch in waters near the Spratly Island group. The three crew members were picked up uninjured by a Vietnamese fishing craft and transported to Nha Trang on the Vietnamese mainland. Within several days, American authorities were notified by the SRV Embassy in Bangkok of the safe rescue of the crew, along with plans for their release several days hence. Such candor and cooperation was a radical departure from previous incidents when Vietnam had arrested Americans and held them incommunicado for extended periods while denying any knowledge of their whereabouts.

One final factor to consider is simply that of elapsed time: the time needed by both sides to dull past pains, ease old animosities, adjust to new ideas, and adopt different attitudes. Indicative of how attitudes have changed with time is the fact that in 1977 most people were put off by Vietnam's request to President Carter's emissary, Leonard Woodcock, for humanitarian assistance from the United States. Many people found the same request much more acceptable when it was made to President Reagan's emissary, General Vessey, ten years later.

Would progress toward resolving the MIA issue be further ahead today had normalization of diplomatic relations been achieved as contemplated in 1978? Or would we instead still be arguing with SRV officials from our little American Embassy compound on Hai Ba Trung Street in Hanoi, trying to negotiate an opportunity to search the countryside, interview villagers, and gather other information about those individuals who are still missing? No one can know.

Could we have done better? In a few small ways, perhaps yes; but considering the political climate and the many factors which have worked against timely resolution of the MIA issue, probably not in any meaningful way. Considering all the time that has elapsed, and comparing what has been accomplished with what is yet to be done, neither the family members nor those who have worked at this effort so diligently can derive much satisfaction from the number of cases so far resolved. The stage is now set for better things, however, and both groups can be justifiably proud of their unwavering stewardship over these many years. They have kept the faith.

NOTES

1. At the personal level, a visitor to Hanoi or Haiphong cannot help but detect a degree of antagonism on the part of the populace toward the Soviets. The origin of this hostility, often manifested by taunts or rock-throwing from Vietnamese children on the streets, is difficult to understand. Since it can be reasonably assumed that Soviet visitors to Vietnam are not routinely mean to children, it seems most likely that the children's behavior must be prompted by attitudes picked up from their parents, elders, teachers, or other adult influences.

2. Department of State message, 85 STATE 176045, DTG 081700Z JUN 85.

3. Vietnamese officials, apparently thinking that a permanent presence in Hanoi was something which the American side wanted, had insisted that it could be permitted only if Vietnam were allowed to have an equal presence in Washington, DC. Once further discussion revealed that American officials were not enthusiastic about placing personnel in Hanoi, both sides jointly acknowledged that the present level of work did not necessitate any immediate consideration of this idea.

4. Reported in a *Washington Post* article on 18 August 1986, as quoted from a release by the Vietnamese News Agency.

5. SRV Foreign Ministry spokesman Trinh Xuan Lang was quoted in a news release filed from Hanoi by the AFP French news service on 29 April 1987.

6. Extracted from the US/SRV statement released jointly by General Vessey and Minister Thach on 3 August 1987 following the conclusion of their discussions in Hanoi.

7. *The Problem of the Disabled in Vietnam*, US Department of State, 13 October 1987.

8. *USCINCPAC Command History, 1988* (TS), vol. II, 29 September 1989, p. 403.

9. American Embassy Vientiane message 2138, DTG 231215Z AUG 88.

10. *Children's Disabilities in Vietnam*, US Department of State, 27 July 1988.

11. *USCINCPAC Command History, 1988* (TS), vol. II, 29 September 1989, p. 406.

12. Ibid., p. 400.

13. *The Washington Post*, 13 October 1990, feature article by *Post* staff writer, Al Kamen.

14. Unfortunately, none of the six remains repatriated from Phnom Penh have yet been positively identified as those of any missing Americans.

EPILOGUE

The US effort to resolve the fate of servicemen missing throughout Indochina continues. A relatively small, but very dedicated group still quietly toils away at this task. Most directly this includes the personnel of the former JCRC which, in early 1992, was absorbed into a newly established organization called the Joint Task Force-Full Accounting (JTF-FA). Also working diligently are the personnel of the CIL, the Stony Beach team, and those—farther removed but still directly supportive of the on-going field activity—in DIA and in the policy-making apparatus in Washington, DC.

The creation of the Joint Task Force-Full Accounting under the Commander in Chief of Pacific Forces is indicative of the heightened emphasis now being directed toward the casualty resolution task. In its first six months of existence the JTF-FA has already grown to nearly 150 personnel from the approximately 40 personnel of the final JCRC days. Small JTF-FA detachments have been established in Bangkok, Hanoi, Vientiane, and Phnom Penh. The organization, now commanded by a Major General, enjoys the very active support of the CINCPAC staff and can draw upon additional resources throughout the DOD as deemed necessary to accomplish its mission.

Organizational changes have also occurred in Washington, DC, with the creation of the office of the Deputy Assistant Secretary of Defense for POW-MIA Affairs. Not only does this office give added visibility to the casualty resolution issue, it serves as a central point for direction of all policy matters on the issue within the DOD.

While the tempo of casualty resolution activity has increased markedly in Indochina, a corresponding increase in misinformation has attracted the attention of the media and added to the public perception that the US government has done little except cover up its sure knowledge that American servicemen continue to be held as prisoners of war. Most notable in 1991 has been the veritable flood of bogus photographs that are alleged to depict specific servicemen still in captivity. MIA activist groups were quick to seize on these photos and began to incorporate them into their fund-raising appeals. One such group included two of these photos in its literature and appealed to its readers as follows:[1]

> Somebody's trying to make it seem as if the men in these pictures never even existed! Let me assure you they not only did, they still do! They're alive today—each one a prisoner of war in Southeast Asia. With hundreds of others, they're victims of the biggest and most disgraceful cover-up in American history!

After four pages of misinformation on this theme, the author then makes his plea:

> . . . I desperately need your financial support. Skyhook II is the only American group working full-time to get our POWs out of Vietnam and Laos while Washington continues to cover up their existence. And it's an expensive struggle . . Our recovery efforts, our face-to-face negotiations with Vietnamese and Laotian government officials, and

all our other efforts on behalf of those POWs and
their families, have exhausted our already meager
funds.

Other critics of the US government have also jumped
into the fray with equal fervor. Under a newspaper headline which states, "Forensics expert identifies MIA photos from Laos," a *Washington Times* writer explains that
a noted anthropologist, forensics expert, and critic of
DOD's identification methods, has identified a man in
two snapshots recently taken in Laos as an Army captain
listed as missing in action from the Vietnam War.[2]

Unfortunately, all of the cited photos have proven to
be fakes. Of necessity, uncounted manhours were di-
verted from more productive tasks to track down the origin and ascertain the true identity of the individuals
depicted in the bogus photos. Equally unfortunately, the
media has taken little note of this fact, leaving the public
with the lasting impression of more government duplicity
and adding to the public belief that hundreds of American
servicemen are known to have been abandoned by our
government in Asian prisons. The purveyors of these
hoaxes have not only played into the hands of those who
are using the MIA issue as a means of garnering funds,
they have once again cruelly played upon the emotions
and hopes of the family members of the missing.

Shortly after the surfacing of the bogus photographs
and the ensuing media attention, a move was begun in
the Senate to investigate once again the possibility of un-
accounted-for American servicemen being still alive in
captivity. On 2 August 1991, the Senate passed a resolution establishing the Senate Select Committee on POW/
MIA Affairs, with Senator John F. Kerry (D-Mass) as
chairman. This committee held a number of hearings
and stirred further controversy because of both its public
pronouncements and its internal squabbles.[3] It remains
to be seen whether, in the long run, this committee will
contribute to clarifying the issue for the American public,
or whether it will only add to the confused public perception and play into the hands of the conspiracy theorists

who are intent on rewriting the history of US efforts to resolve the issue.

As the Vietnam era casualty resolution effort approaches the end of its second decade, all indications point toward serious progress being made. Recent experience leads us to expect that any "backing away" on the part of the Vietnamese, Lao, or Khmer would be but temporary in nature. As noted earlier, the important mechanisms for resolution seem to be in place. The biggest tasks now facing the US side are those of refinement. We need to speed the process and make it more efficient. We must be ready to deal promptly with the inevitable, but not insurmountable, problems which will arise.

This is not to imply that the POW/MIA problem has been solved. The statistics provide ample evidence that resolution still remains far short of the "fullest possible accounting" which the US government has set as its goal. And obstacles will arise, particularly those in maneuvering through the political minefield of relations with Vietnam, Laos, and Cambodia. There will undoubtedly be delays prompted by the tentative relationship with Vietnam, and by a perceived US failure to "create a more favorable atmosphere".

As this relationship builds, however, it is essential that there be a parallel enhancement of trust between the two countries. The work of Presidential Emissary Vessey, a man of abiding decency and honesty, has gone a long way toward dispelling what has hitherto been considerable mutual distrust. The great challenge for the United States now is to continue this movement, to deal forthrightly with former adversaries, and to abandon bitterness and recrimination. Only in this way can we promote the healing process which is still so obviously needed. And only in this way will we give meaning to the sacrifice made by those whose fates we still work to determine.

NOTES

1. Skyhook II Project, headed by former US Representative from New York, Mr. John LeBoutillier, in an undated mailing sent to potential financial contributors in early 1992.

2. *The Washington Times*, 23 July 1991, page A3. Writer Carleton R. Bryant, citing the photo identification work done by Colorado State University professor of anthropology Dr. Michael Charney, says these photos "are the first clear snapshots to be verified by a reputable authority as showing an MIA."

3. Indicative of the confusion which has accompanied the coverage of this issue, following Senate Select Committee hearings on 24 June 92, a 25 June *Washington Post* headline stated "Possibly 80 Vietnam POWs Left Behind, Kerry Says," while *USA Today* published an article the same day carrying a heading which read, "Operation Homecoming in 1973 left 133 soldiers unaccounted for, says Kerry." Chairman Kerry has also had to deal with criticism that his staff, which has included MIA activists holding controversial views, has used the committee to further their own agenda.

GLOSSARY

AP: Associated Press.

ASEAN: The Association of Southeast Asian Nations, comprised of the countries of Thailand, Malaysia, Singapore, the Philippines, Indonesia and, more recently, Brunei.

Bangkok: Capital city of the Kingdom of Thailand.

BNR: Body not recoverd.

CIA: Central Intelligence Agency.

CIL: The US Army's Central Identification Laboratory.

CINCPAC: Commander in Chief of Pacific Forces, located in Hawaii.

CONPLAN: Conceptual Plan.

DIA: Defense Intelligence Agency.

DOD: Department of Defense.

DRV: Democratic Republic of Vietnam (North Vietnam).

FBI: Federal Bureau of Investigation.

FPJMC: Four-Party Joint Military Commission.

FPJMT: Four-Party Joint Military Team.

Hanoi: Formerly the capital city of North Vietnam, now the capital of the unified Socialist Republic of Vietnam.

IAG: Interagency Group.

JCRC: Joint Casualty Resolution Center.

JCS: Joint Chiefs of Staff, located in Washington, DC.

JPRC: Joint Personnel Recovery Center.

JTF-FA: Joint Task Force- Full Accounting, the military organization which replaced the Joint Casualty Resolution Center in early 1992.

Khmer Rouge: The Cambodian communist forces which took over Cambodia in 1975.

KIA: Killed in Action.

League of Families: Common name for the National League of Families of American Prisoners and Missing in Southeast Asia.

LPDR: Lao People's Democratic Republic.

MDE: Media Development Element.

MIA: Missing in Action.

NSA: National Security Agency.

NSC: National Security Council.

Operation Homecoming: Nickname for the military effort associated with the return of the Vietnam era POWs.

OSD: Office of the Secretary of Defense.

Paris Accords: The unofficial name for "The Agreement on Ending the War and Restoring Peace in Vietnam," the agreement which ended the US combat involvement in Vietnam.

PAVN: People's Army of Vietnam.

Phnom Penh: Capital city of Cambodia.

POW or PW: Prisoner of War.

PRG: Provisional Revolutionary Government, the communist "shadow" government of South Vietnam.

PSYOP: Psychological Operations.

PUBCOM: The acronym denoting the Public Communications program to solicit casualty-related information from the local populace in Southeast Asia.

RVN: Republic of Vietnam, the non-communist South Vietnam.

Saigon: Former capital city of South Vietnam, now renamed Ho Chi Minh City.

SEASAL: Nickname for the US Navy's JCRC-directed effort to recover remains of those individuals lost at sea.

SRV: Socialist Republic of Vietnam, created in July 1976 with the unification of North and South Vietnam.
TPJMC: Two-Party Joint Military Commission.
UN: United Nations.
UNHCR: United Nations High Commissioner for Refugees.
UPI: United Press International.
VNOSMP: Viet-Nam Office for Seeking Missing Persons.
Vientiane: Capital city of Laos.

INDEX

Aircraft shot down. See also
    Crashsites
  clues to, 77
  F-8F Crusader, 126
  International
Commission for Control and
Supervision helicopter, 8
  observation planes, 14
  threats, 8
  UH-1B helicopter, 32
  USAF C-5 evacuation,
    28
  North Vietnam missions,
    44
Amerasian children, 178
American Legion, 100
Americares, 168
Amputees, Vietnamese, 159-
    60, 169
Anti-war activism, 2, 73
Armitage, Richard, 91-92,
    127-28, 129, 132,
    143, 146-47, 153,
    154
ASEAN countries, 92, 128

Baker, James, 172, 177
Bangkok Post, 109
Bangkok, Thailand, 74, 86-
    87, 107-08, 128
Bates, Carol, 51
Barber's Point, Hawaii, 49
Brzezinski, Zbigniew, 51-52
Bunker, Ellsworth, 7, 20
Burke, Herb, 57-58
C-130 liaison flights, 8

Cambodia,
  JCRC in, 13, 176-77
  repatriation of remains
    from, 176-77
  SRV invasion of, 62-63,
    74, 84, 87, 151
  SRC withdrawal from,
    172
  US diplomatic relations
    with, 177
Camp Davis, 7
Can Tho City, 19, 29, 80-81
Carlucci, Frank, 156
Carter administration, 50,
    51-60, 61, 63-64, 87-
    89
Casualties, xx
  last Americans, 29
  overwater losses, 15-16,
    32
  Vietnamese handling of,
    83
Casualty resolution efforts.
    See also Joint
    Casualty Resolution
    Center
  accident during, 149
  continuing efforts, 183-
    86
  criticisms of, xxi-xxii,
    54-55
  field work, 133-42, 149
  managed disinformation
    efforts, 111-12
  normalization of
    relations and, 60, 64

post-war support for, 35-
36
priority cases, 158, 169-
70
progress of, 142-47, 166-
76
public support for, 83
refugee interviews, 71-
73
retrospective view of,
177-80
reward money, 117-20
SRV Plan, 146-47, 155
Cease-fire, 5-6, 8, 21, 27
Central Intelligence Agency
(CIA), 75
Child disabilities,
Vietnamese, 160,
169
Children's Defense Fund,
51, 147
Childress, Richard, 135, 153
China
normalization of US
relations with,
63-64
refugees from Vietnam,
74
CINCPAC
CONPLAN 5119, 31
JCRC and, 26-27, 37,
64-65, 88-89
JTF-FA and, 183
rewards program, 18
Congress. See US Congress
Costs
rewards for information,
18-20
SEASAL effort, 16
Crashsites. See also specific
locations
aircraft identification
problems, 164

ambush of field search
team, 22-26
Army OV-IA Mohawk,
167
B-52, 136-40
C-130, 141-42, 143, 166
joint investigation, 134-
35, 136-40, 158, 161-
64, 169-71
Laos, 166-68, 170, 176
National League visits
to, 97
post-war visits to, 134
RF-8G Navy fighter-
reconnaissance
aircraft, 168
selection of, 13, 15, 143
witness interviews, 165
Council for Mutual
Economic
Assistance
(COMECON), 63

Danang, 43
Dean, John Gunther, 177
Defense Intelligence Agency
(DIA), 42, 75, 76,
77,79, 85, 88, 91, 96-
97, 98, 103, 173-74,
175
Democratic Republic of
Vietnam (DRV), 2,
5
economic assistance
demands from US,
43-44
evidence of MIAs, 3-4
delaying tactics, 7-8, 13-
14, 26, 30-31
post-war contact with,
36
and rewards program, 20
US accusations of

treachery,23, 25
Department of Defense
    Assistant Secretary for
        POW/MIA Affairs,
        184
    Assistant Secretary for
        International
        Security and
        POW/MIA Affairs,
        39, 59, 88, 128
    Next-of-Kin Newsletter,
        91
Department of State, 75, 88
Deserters, 50, 56
Died in captivity
    DRV definition, 30
    list, 10
    repatriation of remains,
        9, 64, 126, 157
Dillon, David A., 32
Disinterment, Vietnamese
        customs, 9-10, 85
Dinh Ba Thi, 62Disabled
American Veterans, 100
Dodge, Ronald, 125-26, 148
Dong Ha, 27
Draft dodgers, 50, 61

Easter (Tet) Offensive, 2, 32
Edelman, Marian Wright, 51

Families of MIAs
    advocacy, see National
        League
    distrust of Carter
        administration, 64,
        66, 87
    notification of, xx
    pressure on Paris Peace
        negotiations, 2-3, 4,
        95
    Select Committe report
        and, 47-48, 52

support for casualty
        resolution mission,
        35-36
    testimony before
        Congress, 42
FBI, 62
Ford administration, 42, 50,
        87
Foreign Service of Vietnam,
        53
Four-Party Joint Military
        Commission
        (FPJMC) ambush
        accusations, 23, 25
    effectiveness of, 6, 177
    evacuation, 29
    JCRC coordination with,
        12, 13-14, 18, 21-22,
        26
    mission, 6-7, 12
    representatives, 5, 7
    stalling by DRV and
        PRC, 7-9, 12-13,
        26, 123
    US delegation, 7, 30
Fraudulent fund-raising
        schemes, 101-03,
        107-08, 184
Fryer, Bennie L., 9-10

Garwood, Robert, 43, 53, 86
Gay, Arlo, 43, 78
Gayler, Noel, 18
Gia Lam (town), 76
Gia Lam Airport, 8, 52, 55,
        62
Gilman, Benjamin, 41, 46,
        57, 65
Gooding, Frank, 58
Gougelmann, Tucker, 80
Graf, John, 79-80
Gravesites
    Chi Hoa cemetery, 33

location of, 14, 33, 143,
145
Griffiths, Ann, 156
Gritz, James "Bo," xxi, xxiii,
106-07
Guyer, Tennyson, 46

Haiphong, 134
Hanoi
Armitage delegations,
91-92, 127-28,
129, 132, 143,
153, 155
C-130 liaison flights, 8
Childress visit to, 135,
153
City Directorate of
Cemeteries, 84-85
JCRC Liaison Office,
12-13, 173
Montgomery's
delegations, 42-43,
62, 65, 68, 84
National League visits
to, 97
Paul Doumer bridge, 52
Presidential Commission
to, 50; see also
Woodcock
Commission
records research in, 174-
75
special presidential
emissary to, 155-58,
172
Wolff delegation to, 86,
124
Harvey, Joe, 140
Hawaii
Laotian delegates, 170
SRV delegation's visits,
62, 92, 124, 127-28,
160-61

Hmong, 74, 141
Ho Chi Minh City, 104
Ho Chi Minh trail, 167, 175
Hoa Binh, 134
Hoang Bich Son, 145-46
Holbrooke, Richard, 61, 62
Hong Kong, 74, 84, 85
House of Representatives
POW/MIA Task Force,
92
Subcommittee on Asian
and Pacific Affairs
(Committee on
Foreign Affairs), 57,
86, 103, 107
Hué, 32, 165
Human rights violations, 58
Humanitarian relief, 158-60,
166-67, 168, 176,
180

Indonesia, 74, 92
International Commission
for Control and
Supervision (ICCS),
8
Isom, Harriet, 168

Japan, 74
Johnson administration, 1
Joint Casualty Resolution
Center (JCRC)
activation, 10-11
American embassy and,
17-18
chain of command, 88-
89
CINCPAC and, 26-27,
37, 64-65, 88-89
commander, 11, 15, 25,
27, 49, 130, 143, 156
conceptual plan, 31
congressional review, 40-

41, 42
crashsite visits, 134, 135,
136-38
evacuation of, 29, 32-33
field work, 133-42
FPJMT liaison with, 12,
13-14, 18, 21-22, 26
headquarters, 12, 27, 28,
37-38, 39, 49, 49
Joint Chiefs'
recommendations,
27
joint field work with
VNOSMP, 134-35,
136-40, 158,161-62,
169-71, 173
last operation, 28-29
Laotian delegation to
Hawaii, 142
Liaison Offices, 12-13,
49, 74, 86-87, 107-
08, 173-74
Media Development
Element, 17
meetings with
Vietnamese officials,
123-30
mission, 11, 31, 38, 173
morale, 49-50
Negotiations Assistance
Division, 37, 49
OSD planning
conference, 38
parent group, 156
personnel and
organizational
structure, 11-12, 28-
29, 32-33, 36-37, 38
post-war problems, 35-
36, 88-89
private POW rescue
operations and, 108-
09

public communications
(PUBCOM)
program, 17-20, 28
reduced operations, 26-
29, 36-37, 38
refugee interview
program, 71-83, 96-
97, 104
remains recovered by,
26, 125-26
rewards program, 18-20
search and recovery
operations, 11, 13-
15, 21-26, 28-29,
137-39
sea salvage operations,
15-16
South Vietnamese Army
efforts, 25-26, 28
SRV delegations' visits,
62, 92, 124, 127-28
technical meetings with
SRV, 124, 130-33,
136-37, 146, 147,
151-52, 155, 157-58,
169
Vietnamese counterpart
organization, 124
and Woodcock
Commission, 52
Joint Chiefs of Staff
Chairman of, 155
JCRC and, 27, 88
Joint Personnel Recovery
Center (JPRC), 11-
12, 31
Joint Voluntary Agencies
(JVA), 73
Joint Task Force-Full
Accounting (JTF-FA), 183
Judge, Darwin L., 33
Justice Department, 75

Kamm, Greg, 113, 114, 115
Kennedy, Edward, 33, 44
Kerry, John F., 185
Khanh Hoa Province, 14
Khe Sanh, 8
Khmer Rouge, 13, 63-64, 84, 172
Killed in action, body not recovered, 45
Kingston, Robert C., 11, 31, 156
Kissinger, Henry, 2, 3, 42, 44, 48
Knight, Billy, 10
Korean War, xxii

Lagomarsino, Robert, 58
Lao Peoples' Democratic Republic (LPDR), 140-42; see also Laos
Laos
    casualty resolution efforts, 92, 166-68, 170, 175-76
    consultative talks, 167-68
    crashsites, 141-42, 166-67, 170, 176
    delegation to Hawaii, 142
    humanitarian assistance, 166-67, 168-69, 176
    JCRC Liaison Office, 13
    joint excavation activities, 135, 140-42, 168, 176
    narcotics control discussions, 168-69
    reconstruction aid, 55, 142-43
    refugee interviews, 140-41
    remains repatriated

    from, 170, 176
    resistance fighters, 97, 107, 109, 112, 114, 115, 140
Leboutillier, John, xxi, xxii
Lecornec, Jean, 80-81
Le Duc Tho, 3
Letters, fund-raising, 102-03, 120-21
Libya, US retaliatory raid on, 128-29
Lloyd, Jim, 47

Malaysia, 74, 92
Mansfield, Mike, 51
McCloskey, Paul, 41, 65
McMahon, Charles, Jr., 33
Medal of Honor Society, 101
Missing in action. See also Casualty resolution efforts
    civilians, 88
    defined, xxii
    dossiers on, 38
    evidence from DRV, 3-4
    information exchange with SRV, 53, 56
    information sources, 71-79
    interest groups, 100-03
    knowledge of Indochinese governments, 81-82
    number of servicemen, xx-xxi
    pay and allowances, 47, 67
    reclassification issue, 45, 50, 58, 59, 67, 87-88
Moakley, John, 46, 47, 48
Montgomery, G. V. "Sonny," 40, 41, 47, 49, 51-52, 54, 58, 62, 65, 68, 96

Muong Phine, Laos, 143,
    166
Musselman, Stephen, 148

Nakhon Phanom
    Air Base, 12, 27
    Provincial jail, 106-07
Narcotics control issue, 168-
    69, 178

National League of Families
    of American
    Prisoners and
    Missing in
    Southeast Asia, 47-
    48
adversarial position, 95-
    97, 127
advertisement and
    rewards initiative,
    96-97
Carter administration
    and, 50, 58-59, 64,
    67, 96
cooperation with
    government, 98-99
criticisms of, 99
delegation to Hanoi and
    Vientiane, 97
diplomatic role, 99, 129-
    30, 147, 156
and fund-raising groups,
    103
and Laotian resistance
    fighters, 97
POW rescue attempts,
    97
private search initiatives,
    97
Reagan administration
    and, 90, 98
Reagan speech to, 93
records declassification

for, 90-91, 98
splinter groups, 101
testimony before
    Congress, 98
value of, 100
National POW/MIA
    Recognition Day, 90
Next of Kin Newsletter, 91
Nguyen Co Thach, 62-63,
    124, 129, 132, 136,
    146-47, 153, 155,
    156-66
Nguyen Duy Trinh, 52, 54
Nicotera, Carl, 10
Ninh Binh, 134
Nixon administration, 1, 2
Nixon, Richard, 44, 48, 61,
    65-66
Noi Bai airport, 137-38, 156,
    163
Non-Commissioned Officers
    Association, 101
Non-governmental
    organizations, 159,
    166, 172
Normalization of US-China
    relations, 63-64, 87,
    125
Normalization of US-
Vietnamese
    relations,
    American "technical
        presence" in Hanoi,
        153, 157
    Armitage delegation, 91-
        92
    Cambodian-SRV conflict
        and, 63-64
    high-level policy
        meetings, 152-53,
        172-73
    House testimony on,
        162

internations lending to,
173
MIA issue and, 52, 55-
56, 64, 88, 91-92,
159
normalization of US-
China relations and,
63-64, 87, 125
Paris talks, 56, 57, 61-62
reconstruction
assistance/
reparations issue, 61,
62
spying incident, 61-62,
68
SRV position on, 151-52
technical meetings and,
151-52, 155, 162-63
trade embargo, 173
travel restrictions lifted,
173
UN (New York) talks,
62-63
Woodcock Commission
and, 55-56, 57-58,
60

Office of the Secretary of
Defense (OSD), 38
Operation Homecoming, xx,
6, 12, 86, 96, 117,
126-27, 157
Operation Smile, 169
Ottinger, Richard, 41, 47,
48, 65

Pakse, Laos, 141
Paris Match, 126
Paris Peace Accords, 11
Article 8(b), 4, 7, 8, 9,
20, 27, 30, 38
Article 21, 43-44, 54, 65
Cambodia, 177

cease-fire and, 5-6
communist attitudes, 6,
21, 25, 27
effectiveness of, 179
Kissinger-Le Duc Tho
negotiations, 2, 30
MIA families and, 2-3,
4, 95
MIA issue, 2-3
military commissions,
see Four-Party Joint
Military
Commission; Two-
Party Joint Military
Commission
North Vietnamese
negotiating style, 1-,
30
restrictions on US
personnel in Vietnam,
12
rewards program and, 18
secret negotiations, 2
signatories, 4
terms of, 3
title, 4
US goals, 1-2
Paris talks
normalization of
relations, 56, 57, 61-
62
reconstruction aid, 54,
58, 61
spying incident and, 61-
62, 68
Pathet Lao, 13, 35, 141
Paulson, A.G., 107
PAVN units, 175
Peace Corps volunteers, 114
Perot, H. Ross, xxi, xxiii
Petrie, George, 32
Pham Van Dong, 41, 43, 44,
48, 52, 54, 65

Phan Hien, 41, 43, 44, 52, 53, 61, 67
Philippines, 74, 92
Phnom Penh, Cambodia, 13, 35, 176, 177
Pol Pot, 84
POW/MIA Interagency Group, 93, 98, 130
Prisoners of war
    debriefing of, 12
    denial of existence of, 55, 56, 145-46
    escapees, 76, 79
    fraudulent reports of, 112-20, 184
    imprisoned lawbreakers, 106, 149
    JCRC discussions with SRV, 131-32
    misinformation on, 184
    National League rescue attempts, 97
    non-military, 83
    post-war, 43, 45, 86
    private rescue operations, 11-12, 103-09, 114, 141
    released and repatriated, xx
    reward offers, 117-20
    sighting reports, 76, 78, 82-83, 86, 104-06, 132, 175
Provisional Revolutionary Government of the Republic of South Vietnam (PRG), 4, 5, 7
    delaying tactics, 7-8, 13-14, 21, 26
    US accusations of treachery, 23, 25

Quamo, George, 32

"Rambos," 103-09, 118
Reagan, Ronald, 89-90
Reagan administration, 90-93, 103-04, 155, 175
Reconstruction aid
    Laos, 142-43
    Nixon letter, 44, 48, 61, 65-66
    and site excavation efforts, 142-43
    SRV demands, 53-54, 61, 62
Records and recordkeeping, 11
    archival, 174-75
    declassification of, 90-91, 98
    dossiers on MIAs, 38
    information exchange with SRV, 53, 60
    quality of information, 78
    museum documentation, 174
    refugee interview reports, 75-79
    wartime artifacts, 174
Re-education camps, 82, 178
Refugees
    bilateral concerns, 178
    boat people, 74, 84-85
    camps, 70, 72, 74, 75
    "dog tag" reports, 110-11
    ethnic Chinese, 63, 70
    Hmong, 74, 141
    interview program, 71-83, 96-97, 104, 132, 175
    Lao, 74
    motives for providing

information, 78-79,
110-12
National League
initiatives, 96
POW sightings, 132
processing and
resettlement, 70-71,
78-79, 96, 112
reports generated from,
75
volume of, 69-70, 74
volunteer workers, 73
usefulness of
information from,
79-83
Repatriation of remains, 154
amateur efforts, 109-12
buying and selling of
remains, 110-11,
160, 166
from Cambodia, 176-77
civilians, 81
delays by DRV, 30-31,
44-45, 125-26, 127-
28
died in captivity, 9, 64,
126, 157
"dog tag" reports, 110-
11
at fall of South Vietnam,
64
French, 85
identification
considerations, 110,
148, 157, 171-72
joint US-VSNOP
operations, 135-42
from Laos, 167
last casualties, 33, 37-38
Montgomery
delegations' visits
and, 62, 68, 84
number of remains, 155,

159, 166, 170
positively identified, 67,
170
priority cases, 169-70
refusal by Hanoi, 9
stockpiling of remains,
148
UN membership vote
and, 44, 60
Woodcock Commission
and, 53, 59-60
Rees, Richard, 22-25
Republic of Vietnam (RVN),
4, 6, 7, 13
Roche, John P., 58
Russell, B. H., 7
Russia, 62

Saigon
American Defense
Attaché, 28
American embassy and,
17-18
Americans trapped in,
80, 82
cease-fire, 5
Chi Hoa Prison, 80
Cho Lon section, 70
crashsite, 22-26
evacuation, 29, 32-33,
37-38, 69, 80, 82
fall of, 35
FPJMT negotiations, 7
JCRC Liaison Office,
12-13
Seventh Day Adventist
Hospital, 33
Samae San, 27, 29, 37-38, 39
Saravane, Laos, 167
Savannakhet, Laos, 167, 168,
176
Schwab, Robert, 149
Scuitier, James J., 10

Sea salvage operations
(SEASAL), 15-16
Select Committee on
Missing Persons in
Southeast Asia
conclusions, 66, 96
final report, 45-47, 49,
96
formation, 40
hearings, 40-42
Hanoi visit, 42-44
information gathering,
42
members, 41, 42, 51
National League's
analysis, 47-48
repatriation of remains
to, 44-45
task, 40
Senate Select Committee on
POW/MIA Affairs,
185
Shields, Roger, 39, 59
Shultz, George, 92, 128, 142
Singapore, 74, 92
Skyhook II Project, 120, 184
Solarz, Stephen, 103
Socialist Republic of
Vietnam (SRV)
archival records, 174-75
Cambodian invasion by,
63-64, 74, 84, 87,
151
Foreign Ministry, 135
humanitarian assistance,
157, 158-60, 169
knowledge of MIAs, 53,
56, 87, 125-26, 179
normalization talks, 52,
56, 57, 60, 61-62, 88,
151-52
persecution of ethnic
Chinese, 63, 70, 74,

84-85
private American claims
against, 161
technical meetings with
JCRC, 124, 130-33,
136-37, 146-47, 151-
52, 155, 157-58, 162-
63, 169
Treaty of Friendship
and Cooperation
with Russia, 63
UN membership, 44, 58,
60, 61, 66, 178
US influence, 178
visits to Hawaii, 62, 92,
124, 127-28
withdrawal from
Cambodia, 172
Southern Governors
Conference, 44
South Vietnam
died-in-capivity list, 10
evacuation, 28-29
fall of, 7, 13, 28, 29, 37,
64, 81
North Vietnamese push
into, 27
search and recovery
operations, 14-15
South Vietnamese Army
search and recovery
activities, 25-26,
28
soldiers' remains, 14-15,
67
Sparks, Donald Lee, xix-xx,
126, 148
Spratley Island group, 179
Stars and Stripes, 18
Stoney Beach group, 175,
183
Strait, Charles, 116-17

Tam Ky, xix
Tan Son Nhut Air Base, 7,
    22, 28
Tchepone, Laos, 143, 167
Thach. See Nguyen Co
Thach
Thailand, 92
    base closures, 39, 49
    Gritz arrest, 106
    JCRC Headquarters, 12,
        27, 28, 29, 37-38
    Lao refugees, 140-41
    Nakhon Phanom
        Provincial jail, 106-
        07
    Vietnamese refugee c
        camps in, 70, 71
Thanh Hoa, 144
Tombaugh, William, 23, 25
Tran Huu Hai ("Tony
    Hai"), 104-06
Treaty of Friendship and
    Cooperation, 63
Two-Party Joint Military
    Commission
    (TPJMC), 5
Tuy Hoa, 14
Twining, Charles, 177
Ulatoski, Joseph, 25
United Auto Workers, 51
United Nations
    High Commissioner for
        Refugees, 71
    membership of Vietnam,
        44, 58, 60, 61, 66,
        178
    SRV Mission meetings,
        129-30
United States Support
Activities Group, 156
Urbaniak, Roger, 32-33
US Army
    7th PSYOP Group, 17

Central Identification
    Laboratory, 12, 15,
    28-29, 33, 39, 42, 45,
    62, 86, 88, 89, 109,
    111, 130, 167, 183
Corps of Engineers, 176
Graves Registration
    units, 100
US Congress. See House of
    Representatives;
    Select Committee
    on Missing Persons
    in Southeast Asia;
    Senate
US Information Agency, 61-
    62
US Information Service, 20
US Marines
    casualties, 29, 33, 37-38

    Viet Cong collaborator,
        43
US Navy
    salvage operations, 15-16
U-Tapao Air Base, 39, 49

Van Dyke, Richard, 148
Vang Pao, 141
Vessey, John W., Jr., 31,
    155-66, 172, 173,
    180, 186
Vessey-Thach agreements,
    158-66, 172, 173
Veterans of Foreign Wars,
    100
Vientiane, Laos, 13, 42, 50,
    55,68, 97, 141,
    167,168-69
Viet Cong, 4
    ambush of JCRC search
        team, 22-26
    collaborators, 43
Viet-Nam Office for Seeking

Missing Persons
(VNOSMP)
Hawaii visit, 160-61
investigation of POW
sightings, 132
joint field work with
JCRC, 134-35, 136-
40, 158, 161-66, 173
membership, 124, 130
polemic presentations,
132-33
POW issue, 131
remains repatriated by,
127, 160
site selection, 145
technical meetings with
JCRC, 128, 130-33,
146, 151-52, 155,
158, 160, 162-63
training and equipment
for, 157, 160

Vietnam Veterans of
America, 100
Vietnamese people. See also
South Vietnamese
Army
assistance in gravesite
location, 14
rewards for assistance,
18-20
Vinh, 165
Vinh Binh Province, 79
Vollmer, John P., 29

Washington Post, 172
Washington Star, 58
Washington Times, 185
Wolff, Lester, 86, 124, 148
Wolfowitz, Paul, 129
Wood, Tony, 32
Woodcock Commission
controversy, 51-52

criticisms of, 54-55, 56-
58
impact of, 59-60
and information
exchange on MIAs, 53,
60
members, 51-52
mission, 51
National League's
reaction to, 51-52,
58-59, 96
normalization of
relations, 55-56, 57-
58, 60
reconstruction aid, 53-54
repatriation of remains
to, 53, 55, 59-60
report, 55, 57, 59
SRV's areas of concern,
53-54, 58
treatment in Hanoi, 52-
53, 54-55
US public opinion on,
54-55
Woodcock, Leonard, 51, 55,
57, 59, 155, 180
World War II, xxii, 16

Yen Thuong, 136-40
Yost, Charles, 51

THE AUTHOR

Lieutenant Colonel Paul Mather holds a Bachelor's Degree in Aeronautical Engineering from Iowa State University, and a Master's Degree in Mechanical Engineering from the University of Wyoming. During the early years of his military career, he served in engineering assignments related to intercontinental ballistic missiles. Following specialized training with the Army and several tours of duty in Vietnam, he served in Southeast Asia with the Joint Casualty Resolution Center from the time of the unit's creation in early 1973 until his return to the United States in the fall of 1988. He wrote this book, much of it based on his personal experiences, while a Research Fellow at the National Defense University from September 1988 to January 1990. Lieutenant Colonel Mather retired in January 1990 after over 30 years' active duty with the United States Air Force.

☆ U.S. GOVERNMENT PRINTING OFFICE:1994-282-306/40012